THE MASTER'S MUSE

Unicorn Publishing Group LLP
66 Charlotte Street
London
W1T 4QE
www.unicornpress.org

Published by Unicorn Publishing Group LLP 2015

ISBN 978-1-910065-63-1

10 9 8 7 6 5 4 3 2 1

Book design by Felicity Price-Smith
Printed in India by Imprint Digital Ltd

THE MASTER'S MUSE

ARTISTS' CATS AND DOGS

Paintings and Prints by Mychael Barratt

Unicorn Press

In my first year at art school I did a photography project that featured my fellow classmates in poses imitating iconic paintings. This revealed to me a vein of inspiration that I have intermittently returned to ever since.

One day many years ago while working on a piece in a series called *Life Imitating Art*, I started to think about what Marc Chagall's dog might look like and did the drawing for *Chagall's Dog in Love*. This was quickly followed by *Van Gogh's Dog* and a cascade of other ideas in what has become a running series that shows no signs of ebbing.

DAMIEN HIRST'S DOG

Etching and aquatint
22 x 22 cm
2009

When I first discussed plans to do a Damien Hirst themed piece the general reaction was one of horror as people imagined a ghoulish, pickled dog. Fortunately, it was his spot paintings that had inspired me.

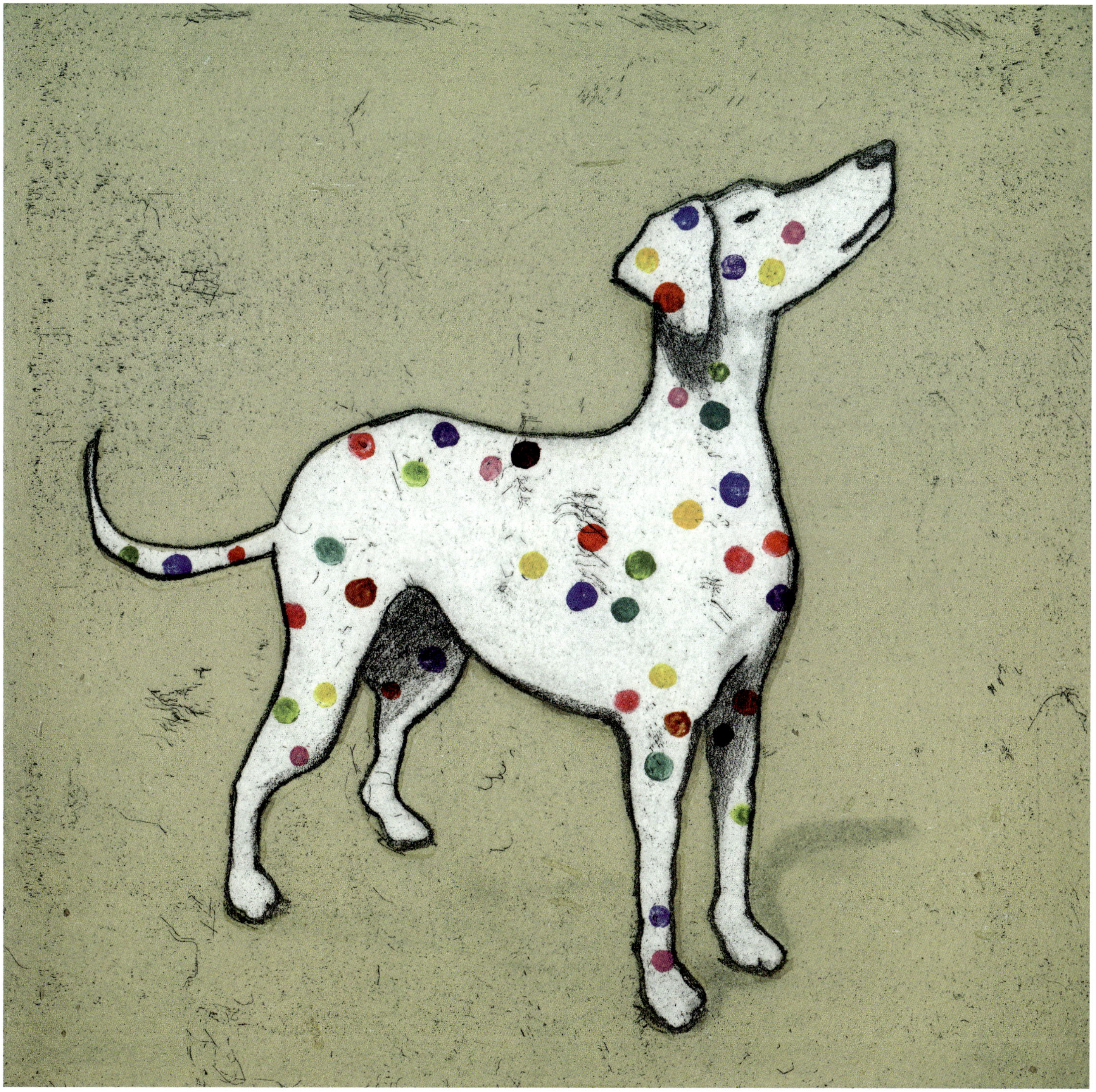

HOCKNEY'S DOG

Etching and aquatint
22 x 22 cm
2008

I created a very simple brief for this piece: to combine one of Hockney's big splash paintings with one of his portraits of his Dachshunds Stanley and Boodgie. One of the only pieces in this series that has been seen by the artist who was the subject.

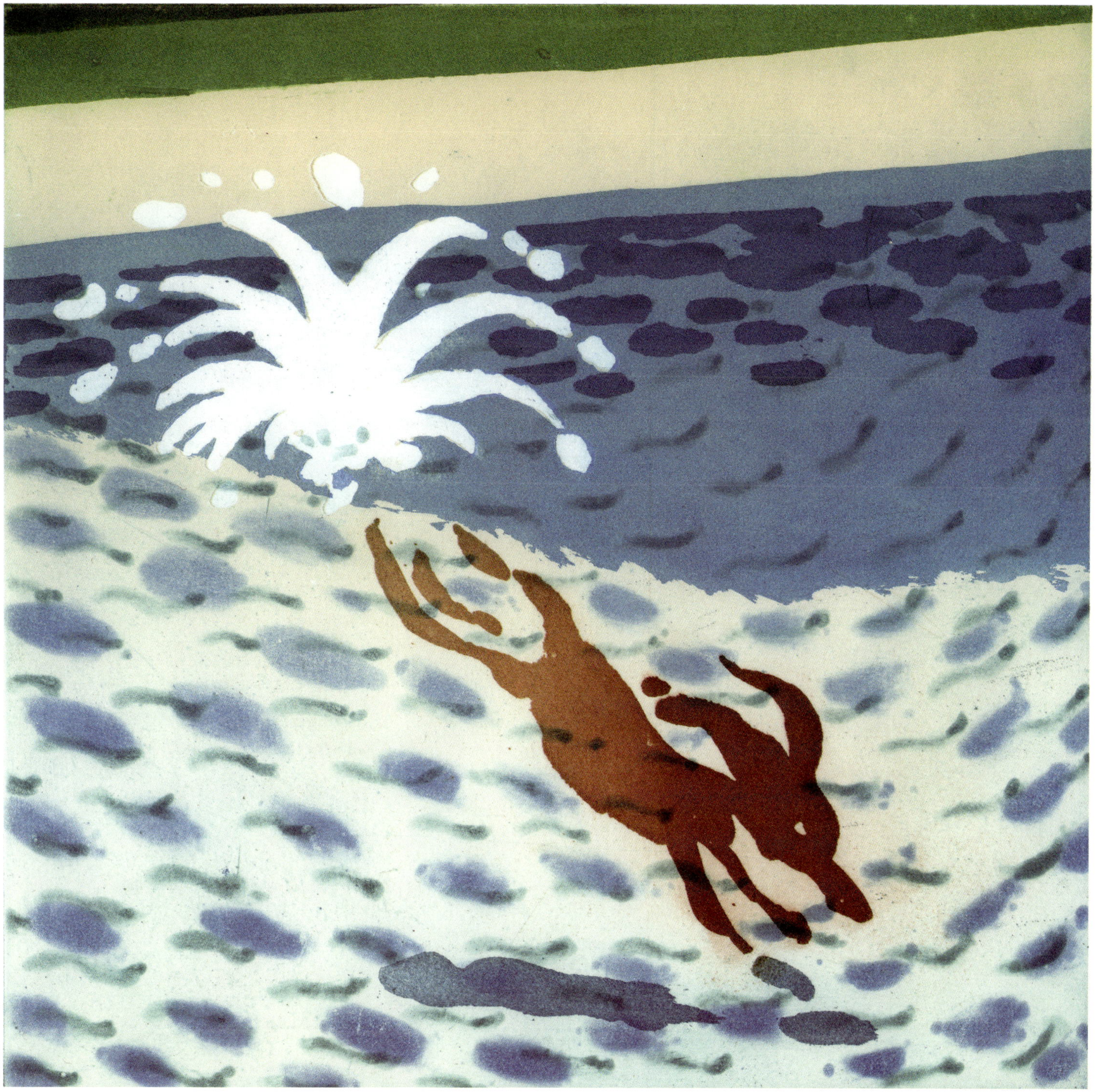

VAN GOGH'S CAT

Oil on panel
40 x 40 cm
2007

This is a case of art imitating life as one of my cats actually did this to the rush seat of my Habitat Van Gogh inspired chair.

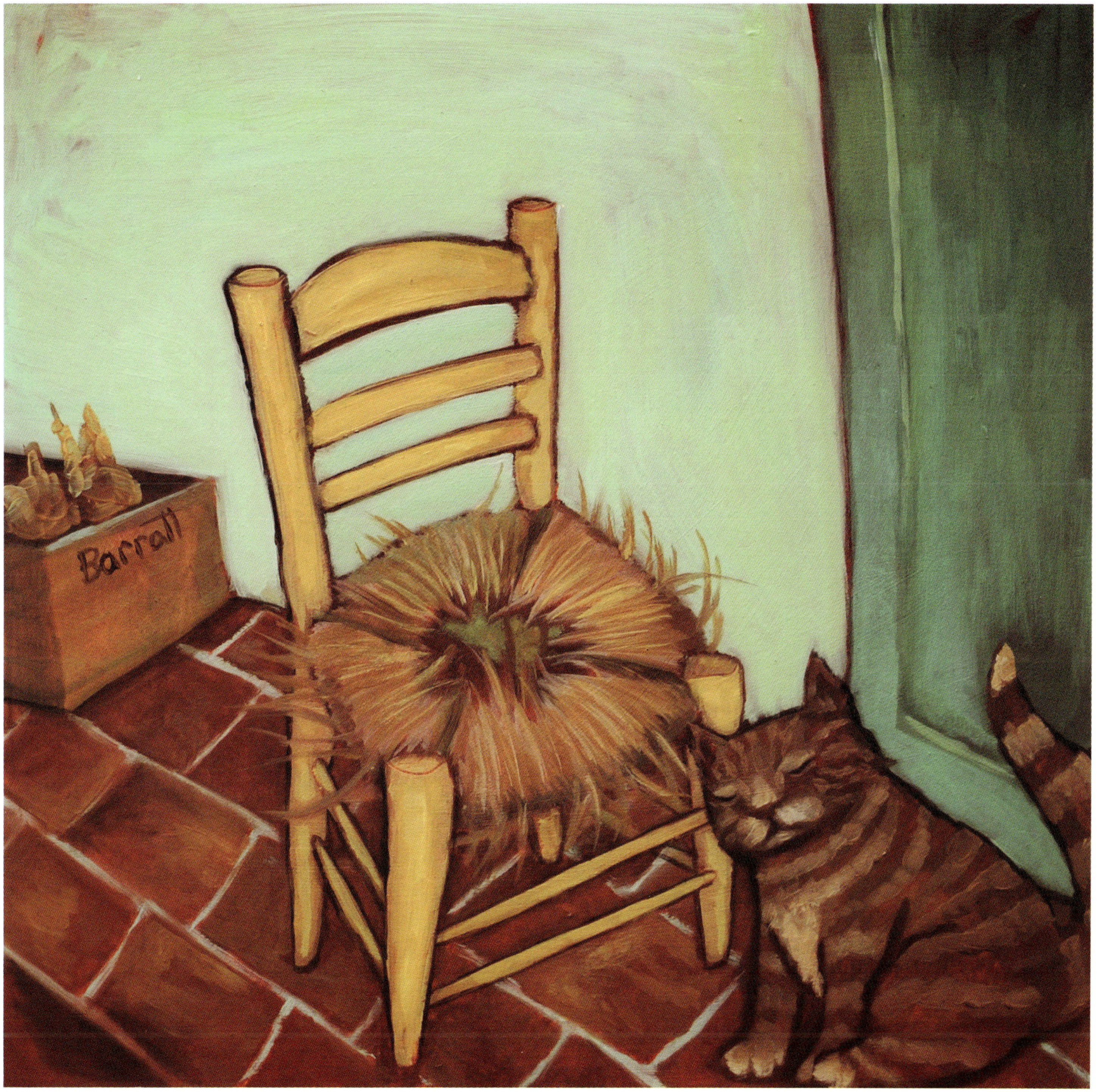
Barratt

LEONARDO DA VINCI'S DOG

Oil on Panel
40 x 40 cm
2013

This one occurred to me while I was looking at *Lady with an Ermine* at the National Gallery, London and includes a portrait of my dog.

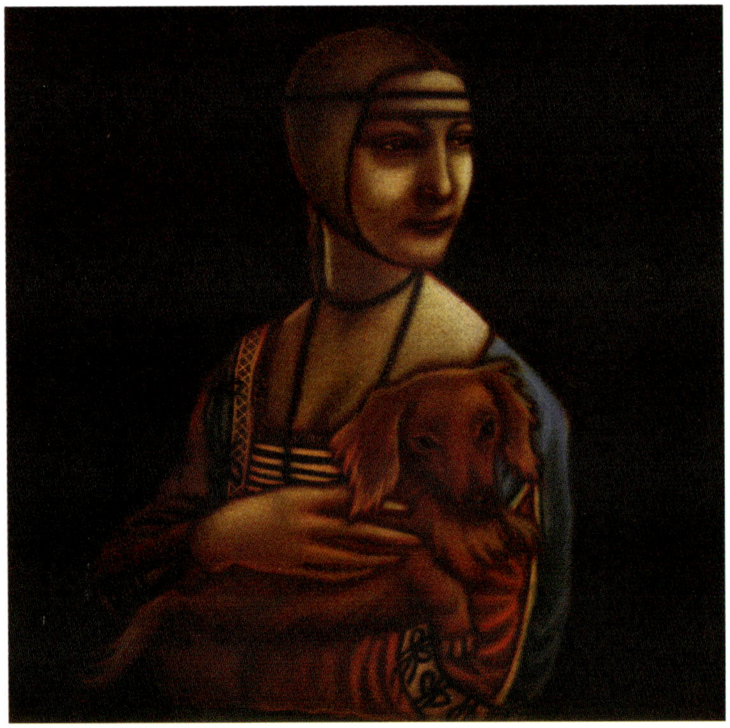

Mezzotint 22 x 22 cm 2013

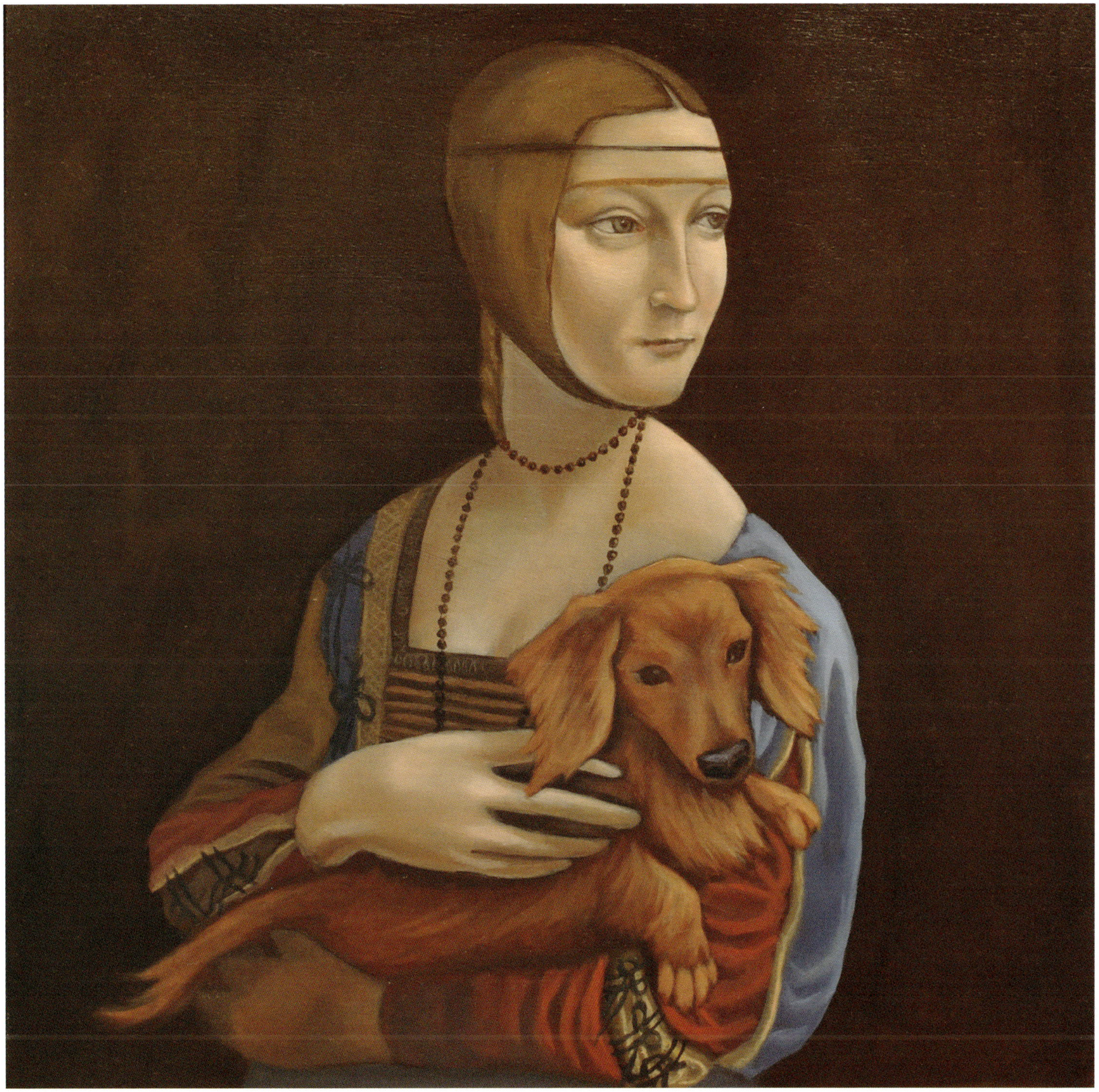

GIACOMETTI'S DOG

Etching and aquatint
22 x 22 cm
2006

I have always felt that this is an obvious reference but it has curiously been the piece most often misunderstood by those who own it. I have been contacted three times by people saying 'I've had Giacometti's dog hanging in my house for a year and I just got it'.

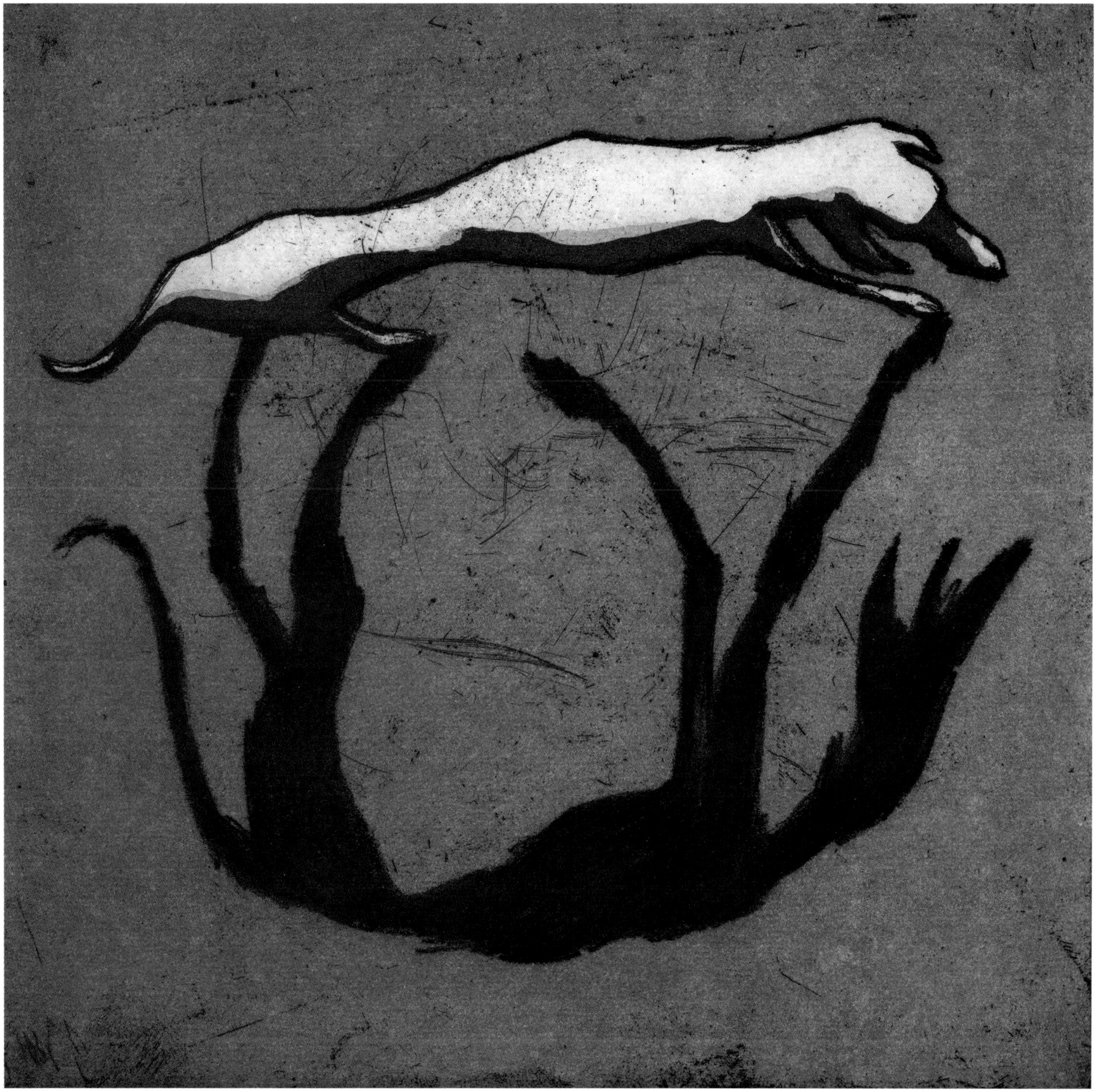

TRACEY EMIN'S DOG

Oil on panel
40 x 40 cm
2009

This piece was inspired by Tracey Emin's most iconic and memorable work *My Bed* although I have slightly tidied up the detritus on the floor.

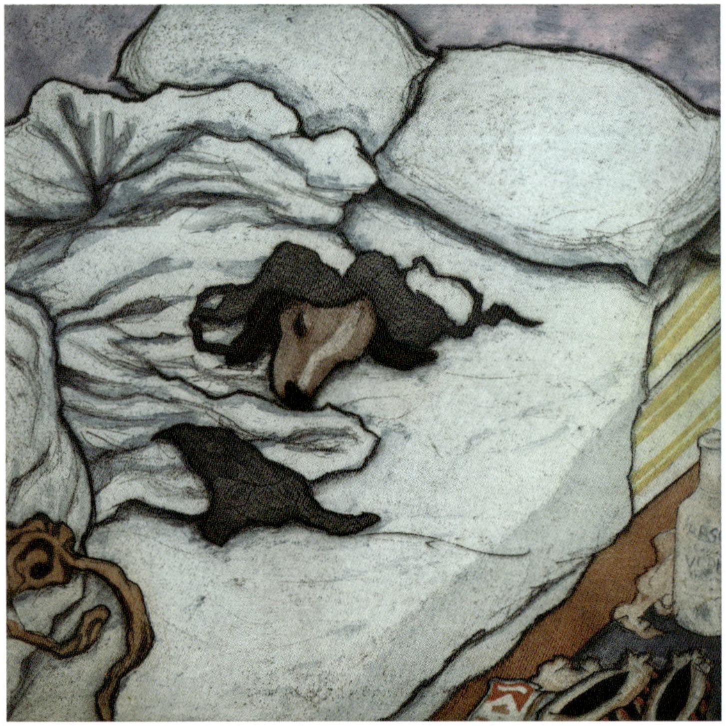

Etching and aquatint 22 x 22 cm 2009

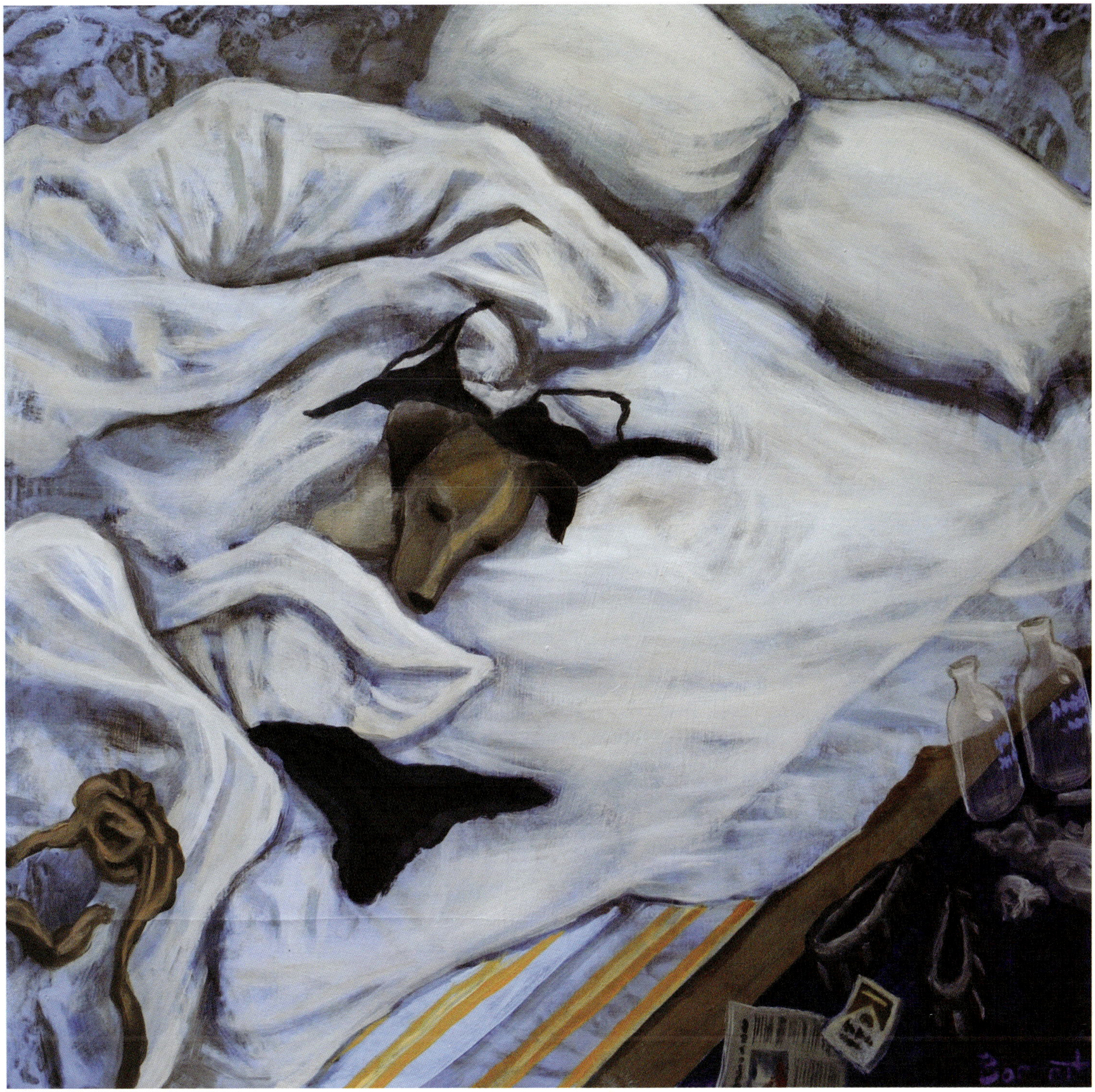

ROUSSEAU'S CAT

Etching and aquatint
22 x 22 cm
2007

This was originally conceived as *Rousseau's Dog* but did not sit well with the artist's style so it became the first piece to include a cat.

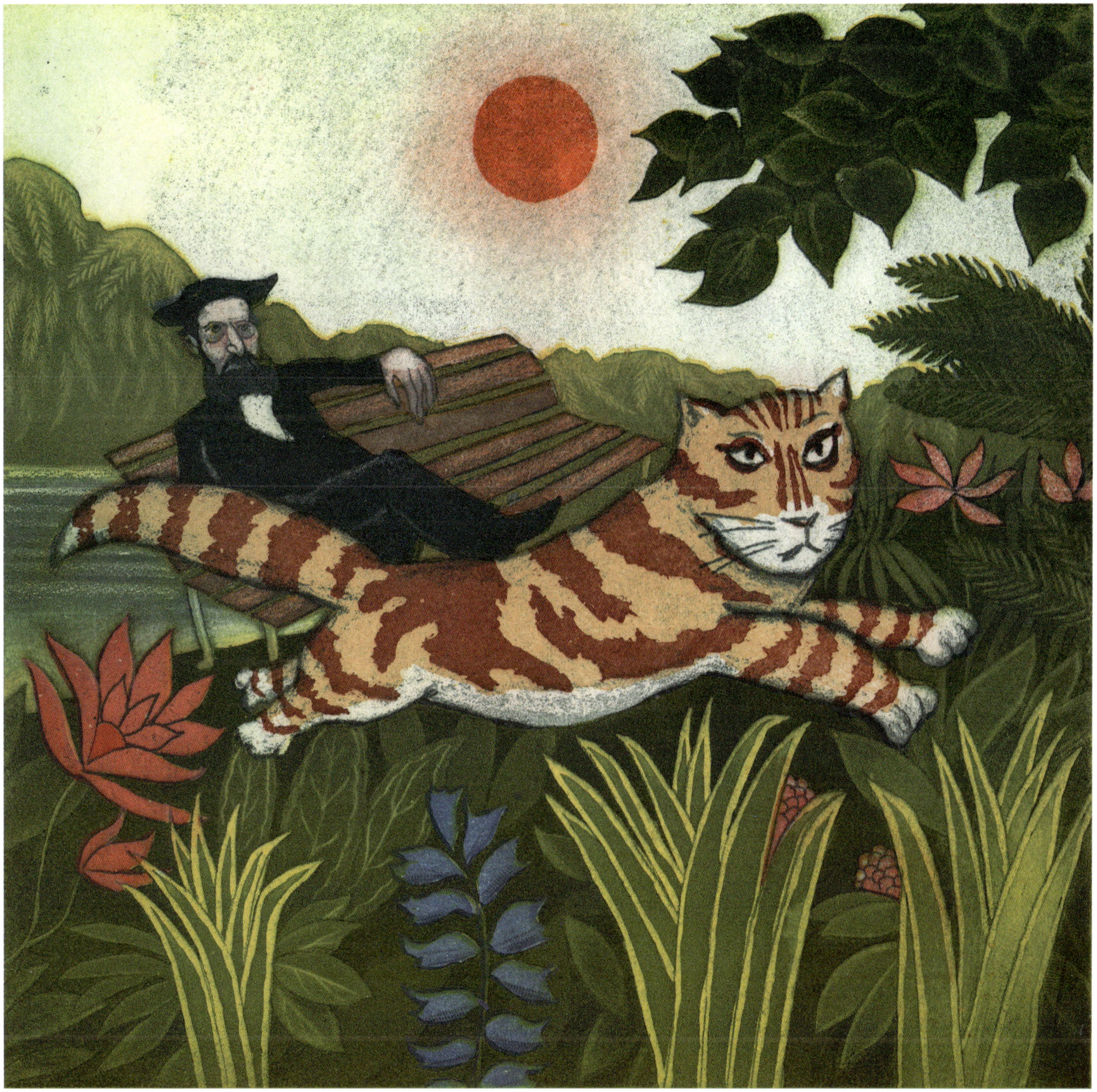

ROTHKO'S DOG

Oil on panel
40 x 40 cm
2015

The idea for the etching was prompted by an offhand joke. A gallery owner was telling me how much she loved this series and asked me which artist was next. I quickly replied 'Rothko' believing him to be so improbable that she would just laugh. When she replied 'Oh wonderful! Rothko is my favourite artist – I can't wait!' I was forced to come up with something. I love Rothko's work myself and do see this as homage but I don't believe that he would have forgiven me for it.

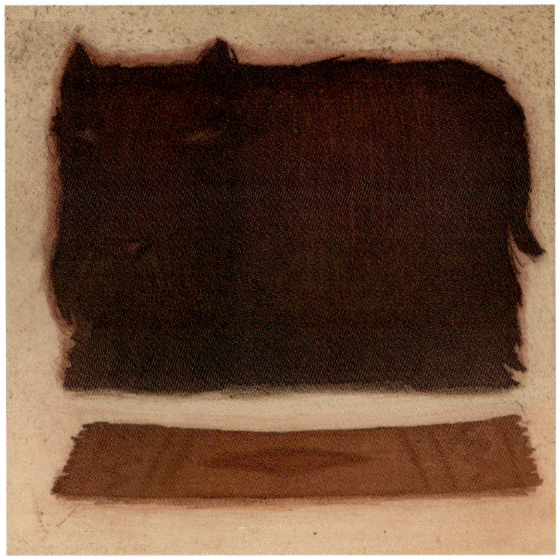

Etching and aquatint 22 x 22 cm 2009

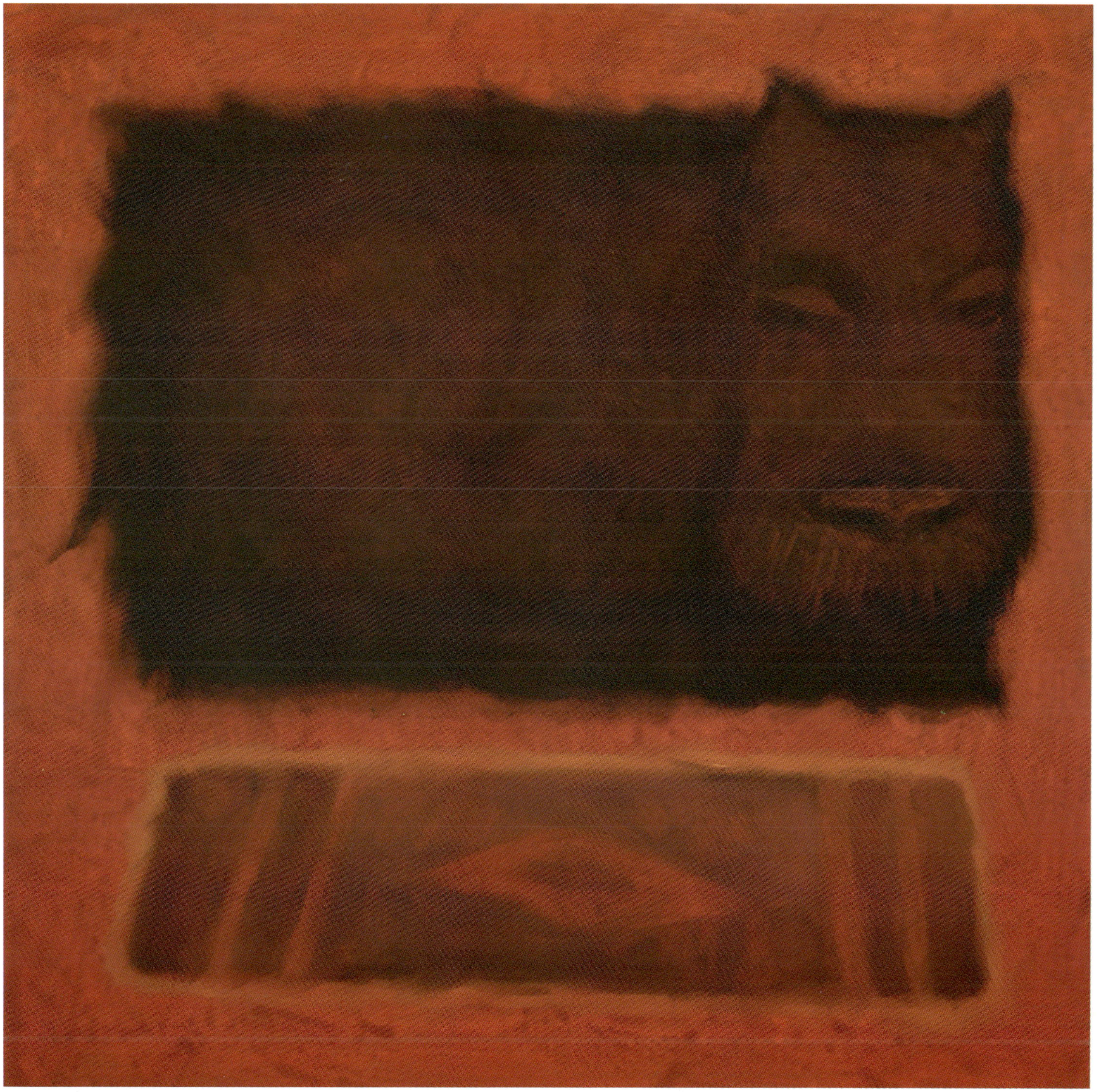

VAN GOGH'S DOG

Hand-coloured etching and aquatint
22 x 22 cm
2004

The second etching in this series, this is one of the few that has an unabashed punch line.

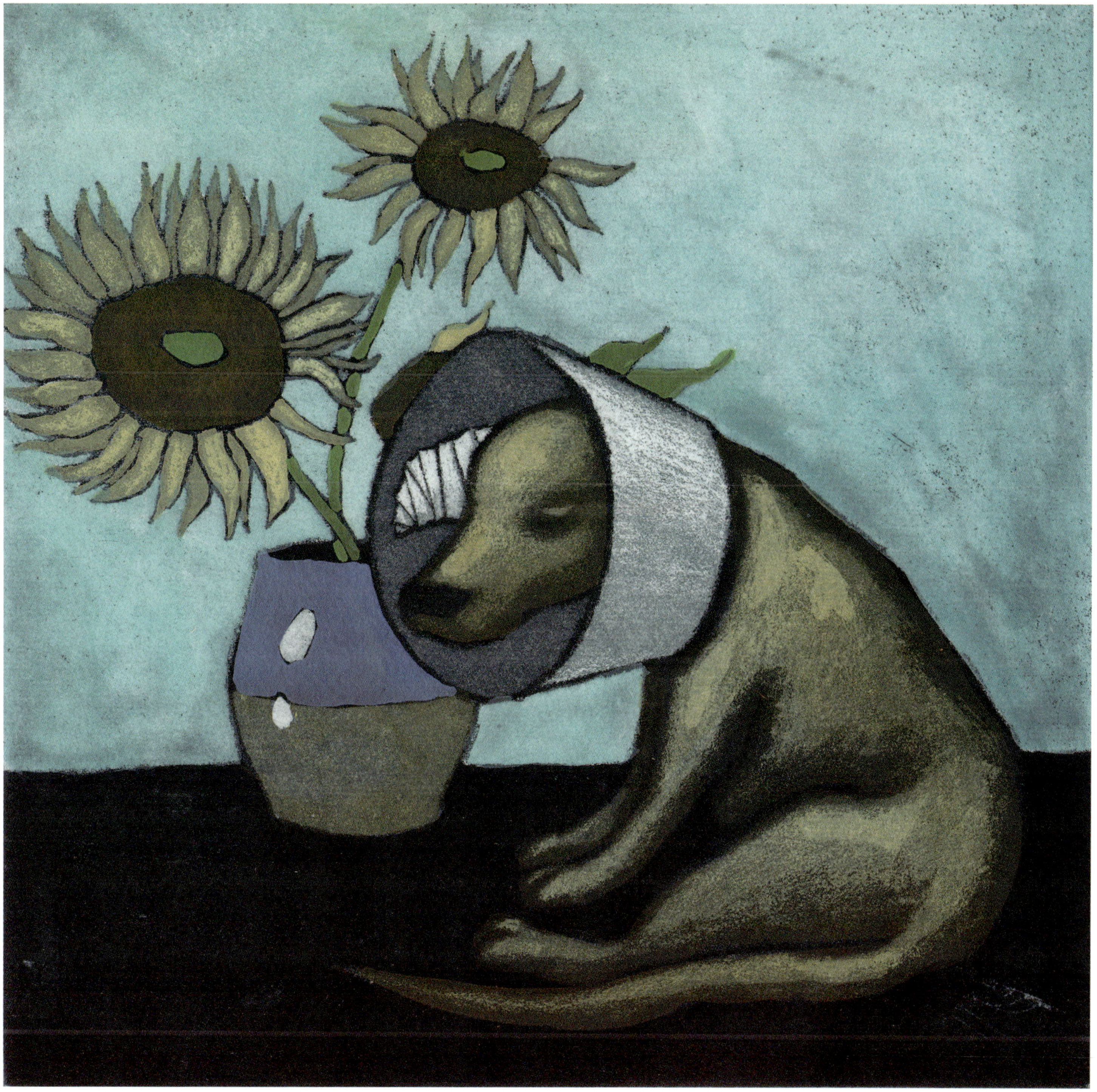

KANDINSKY'S DOG

Oil on panel
40 x 40 cm
2008

For this painting the client requested a piece based on the geometrical abstract work of Wassily Kandinsky; my most challenging commission thus far.

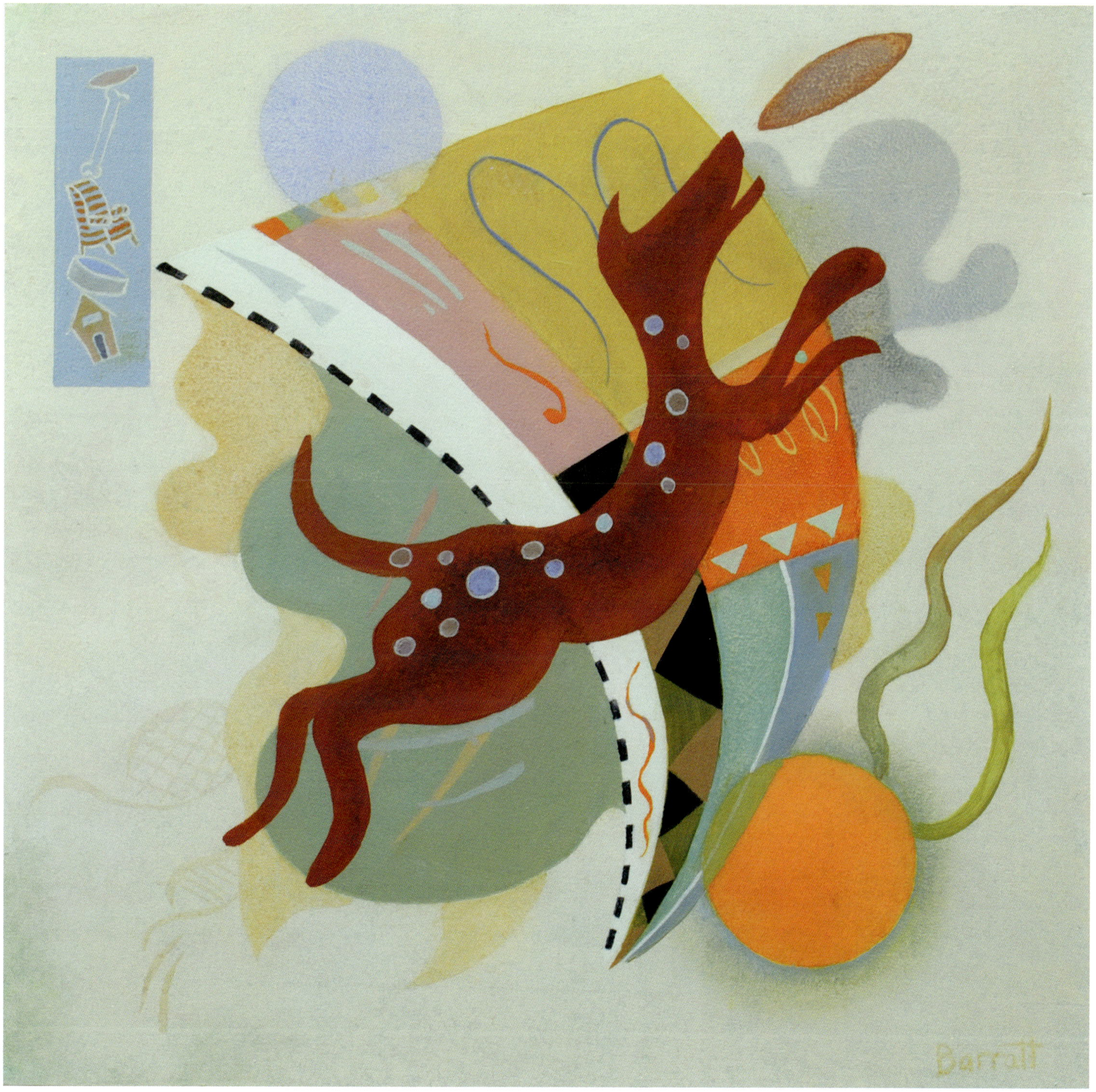
Barratt

DUBUFFET'S CAT

Oil on panel
40 x 40 cm
2008

This painting is an attempt to channel the energy and spontaneity of Dubuffet's pieces like *The Busy Life and Affluence*. Painted shortly after *Kandinsky's Dog*, I often paint these in wildly contrasting pairs.

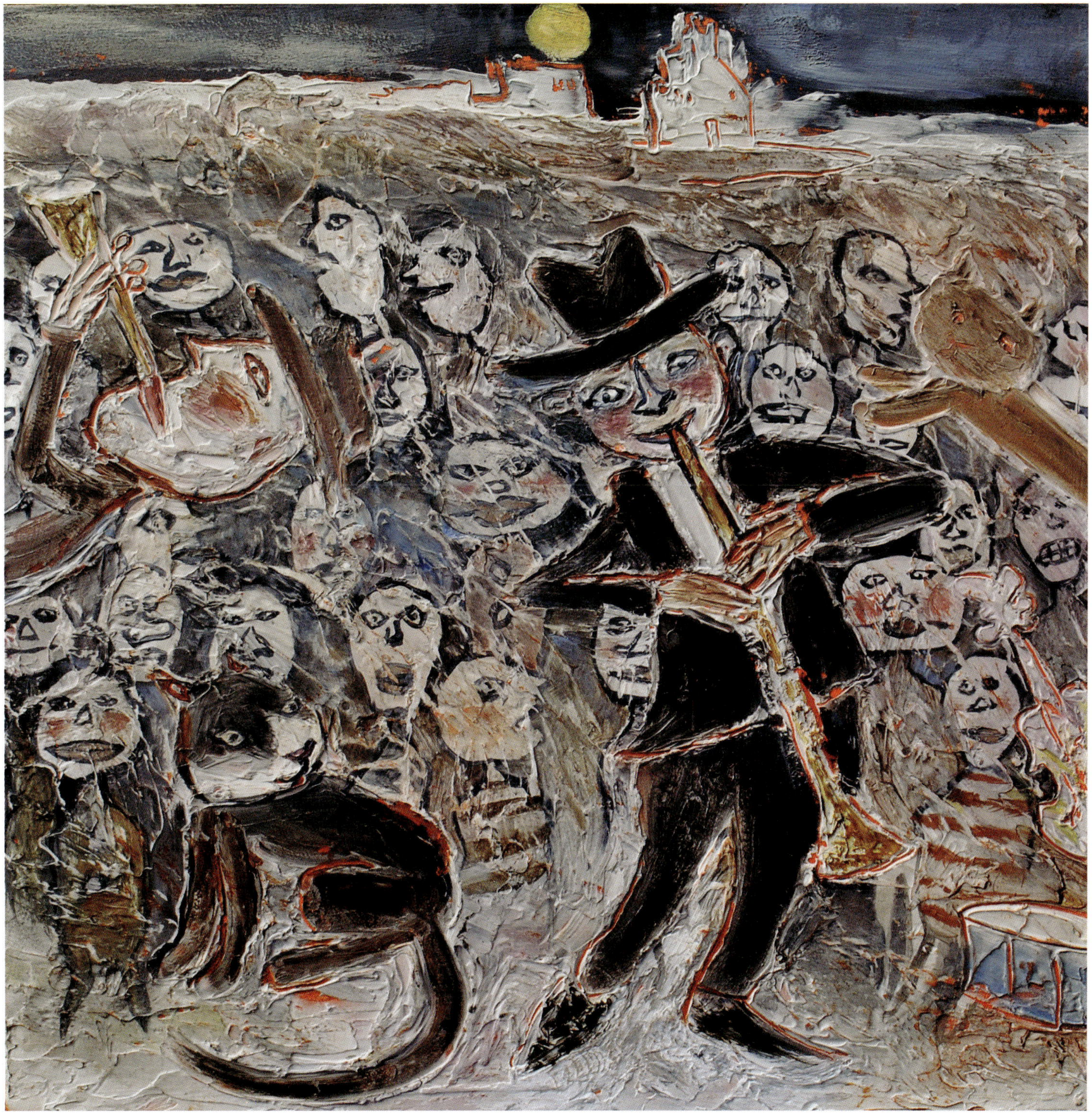

PHILIP GUSTON'S DOG

Oil on panel
40 x 40 cm
2015

I've always loved the shift that Philip Guston's work made from pure abstract expressionism to the cartoonish renderings of objects and people. It was his handling of simple iconic objects like *Shoes* and *The Coat* that particularly inspired me.

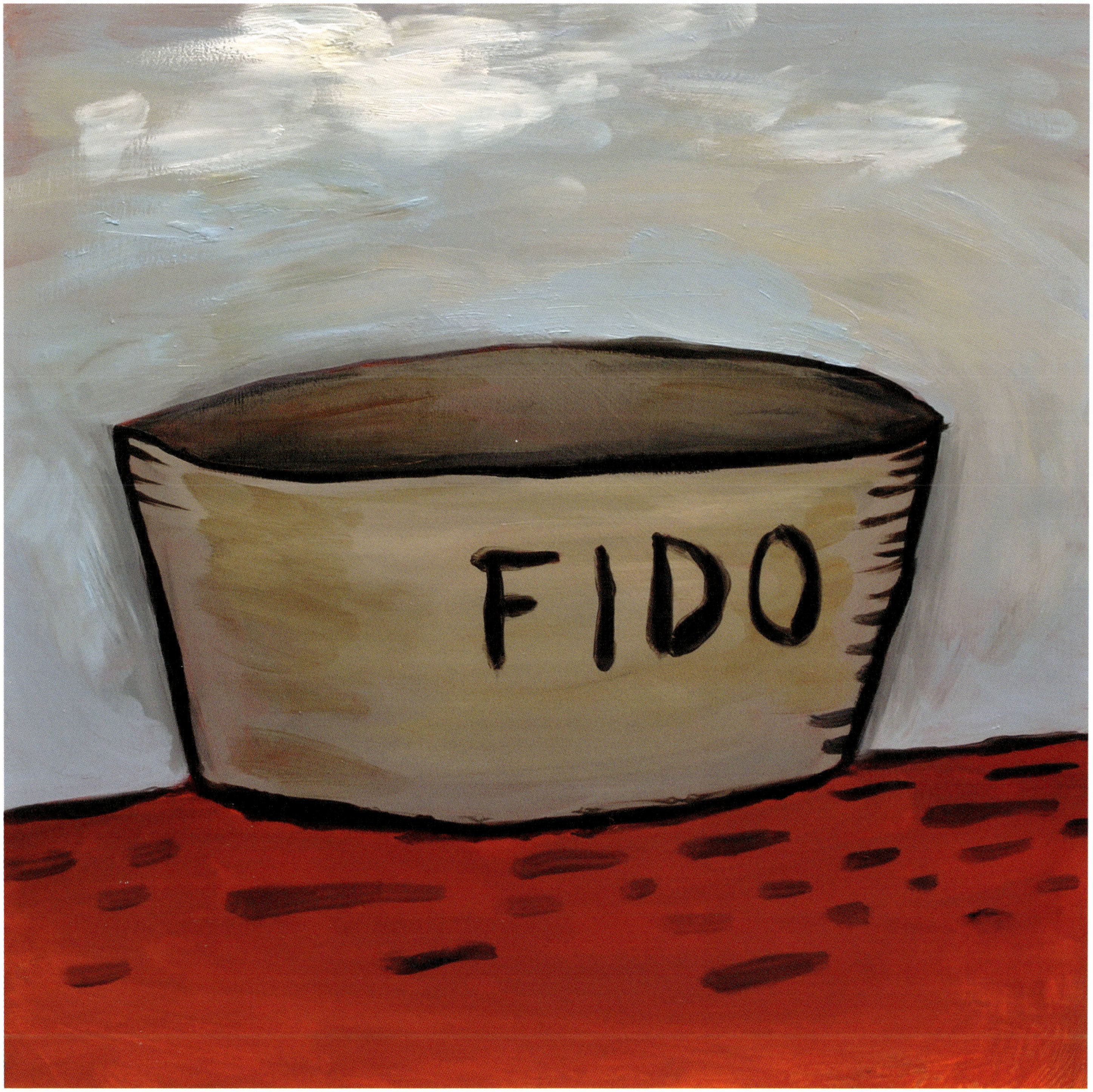
FIDO

MATISSE'S DOGS

Hand-coloured etching and aquatint
22 x 22 cm
2006

This was the last etching I made before the ideas necessitated working with multiple colour plates. The painting I did in oil of the same subject better captures the mood of the original.

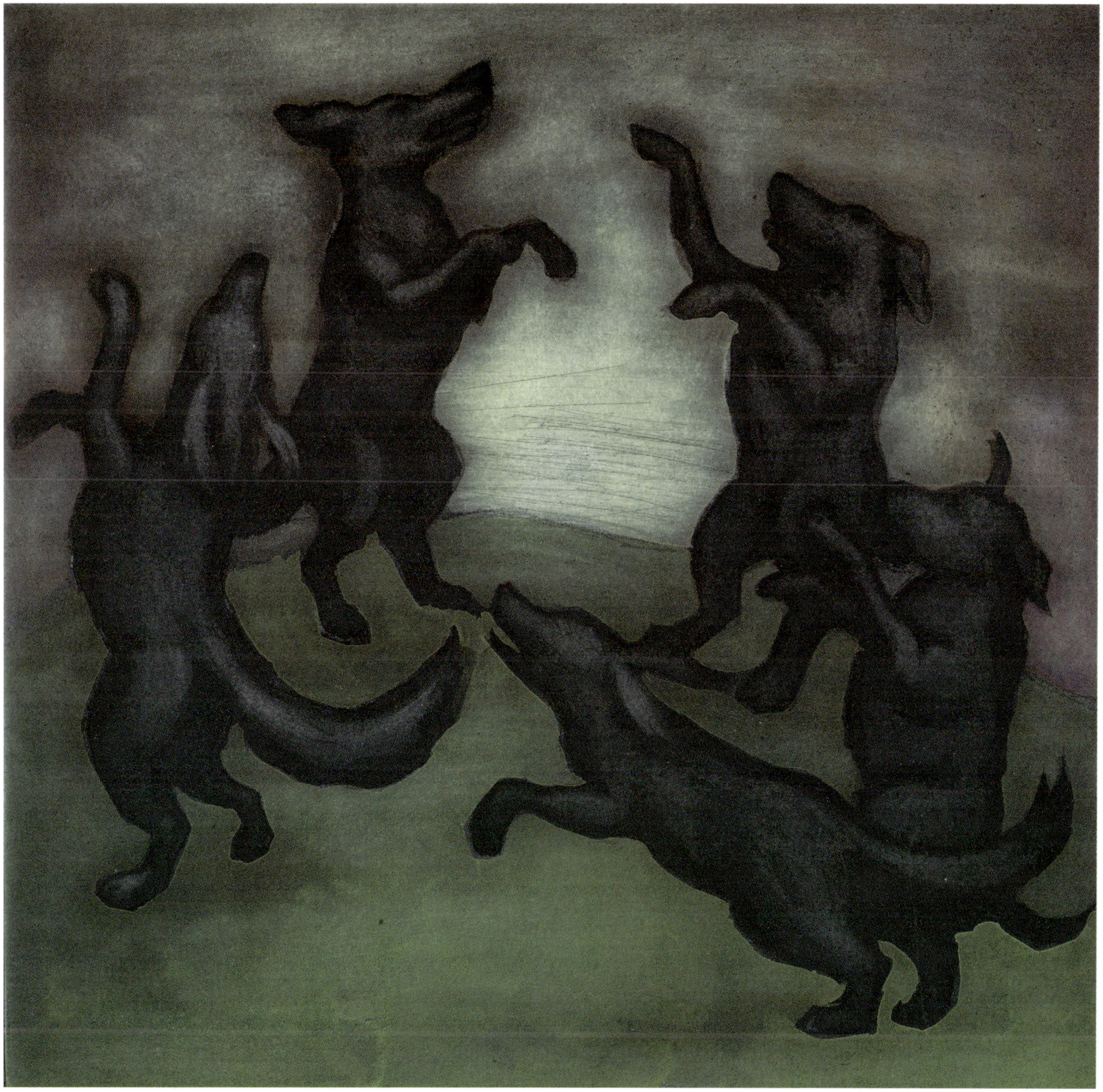

PETER BLAKE'S DOG

Oil on panel
40 x 40 cm
2015

This is based on Peter Blake's painting *On the Balcony* from 1955-7, which is in Tate Britain. I have replaced all of his pop culture and personal history references with dog related ones from the same era. Most of the toys are things I actually remember owning.

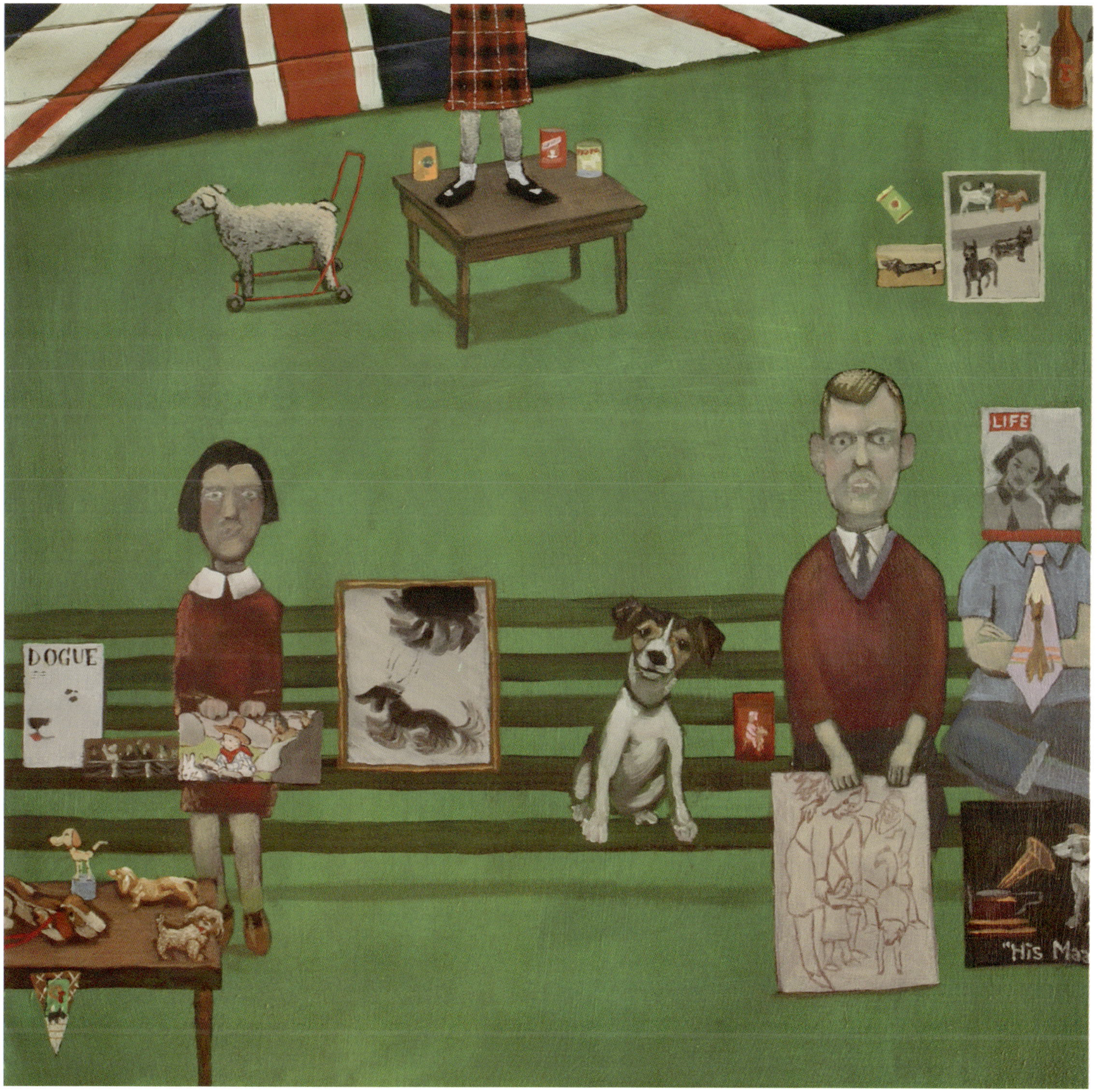
DOGUE
LIFE

RACHEL WHITEREAD'S DOG

Oil on panel
40 x 40 cm
2009

My favourite work by British artist Rachel Whiteread is *House*, a concrete cast of the inside of an entire Victorian house just off the Mile End Road in London. I imagined her working up to that piece with a preliminary attempt to cast her dog's house.

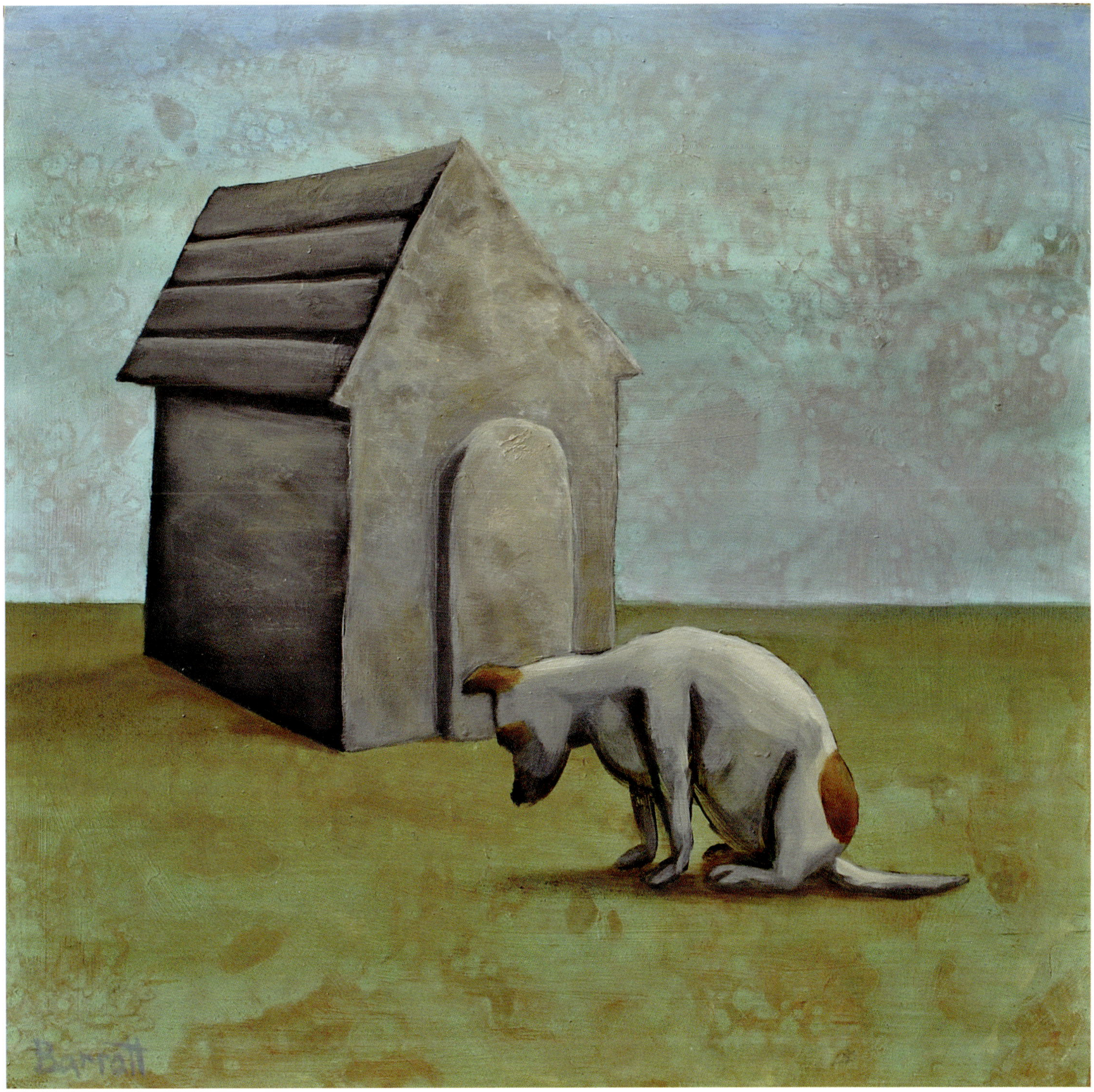
Barratt

YVES KLEIN'S CAT

Mezzotint
22 x 22 cm
2013

The idea for this mezzotint came when one of my cats walked across a painting that I was working on.

MATISSE'S CAT

Oil on panel
40 x 40 cm
2010

Based on Matisse's painting *The Goldfish*, this is a familiar scenario to anyone with cats and fish.

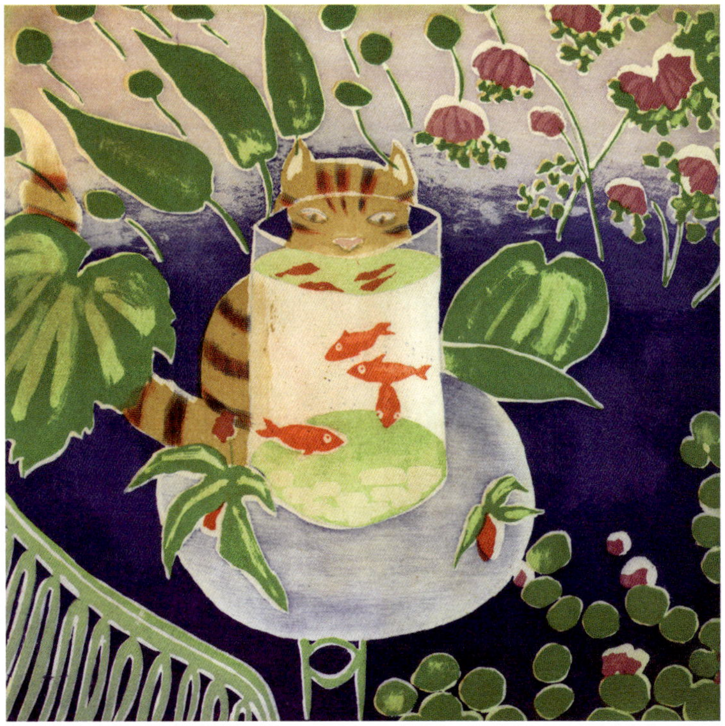

Etching and aquatint 22 x 22 cm 2010

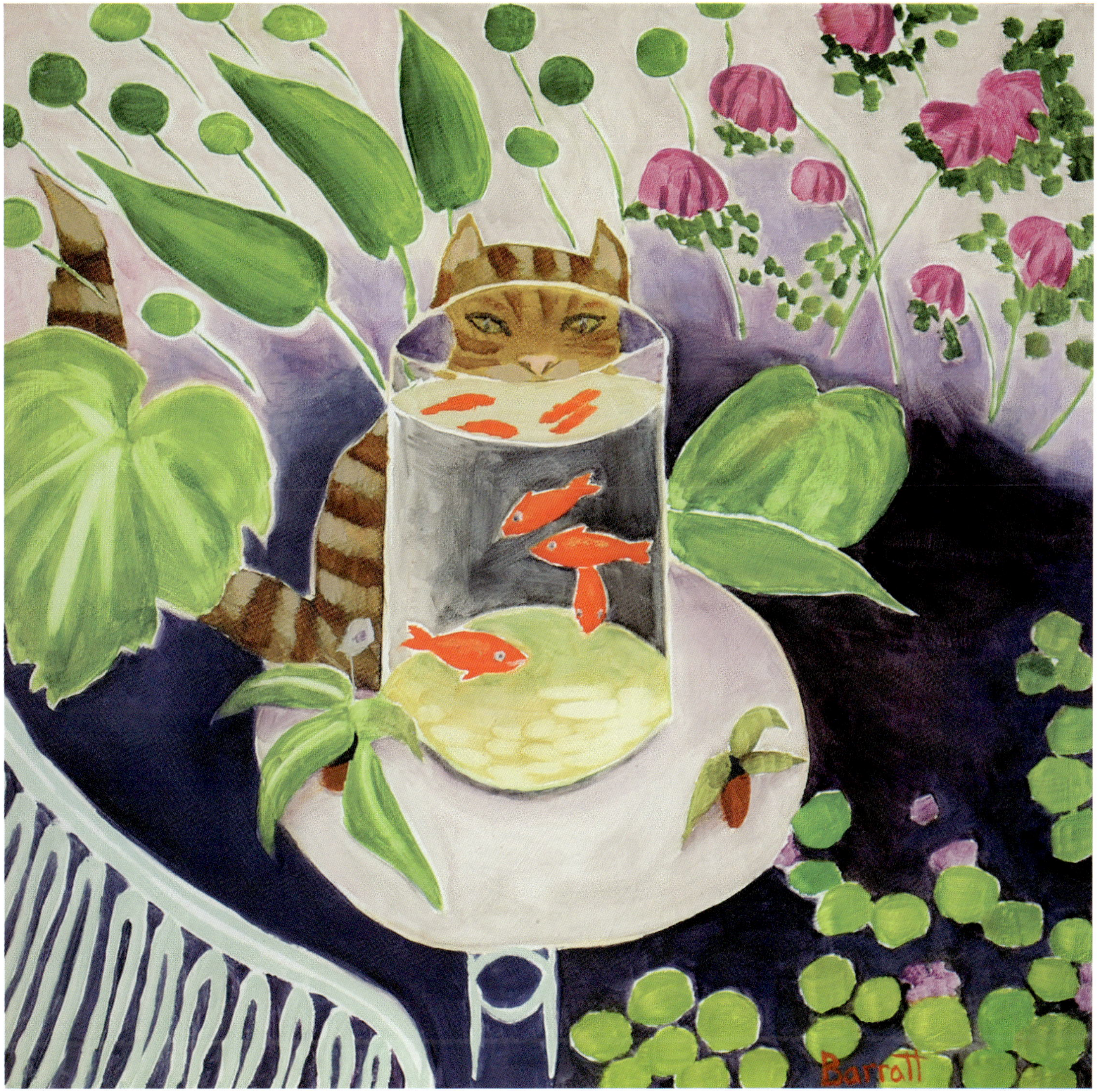
Barratt

MODIGLIANI'S DOG

Hand-coloured etching and aquatint
22 x 22 cm
2005

This etching was an attempt to translate Modigliani's style of portraiture to a dog.

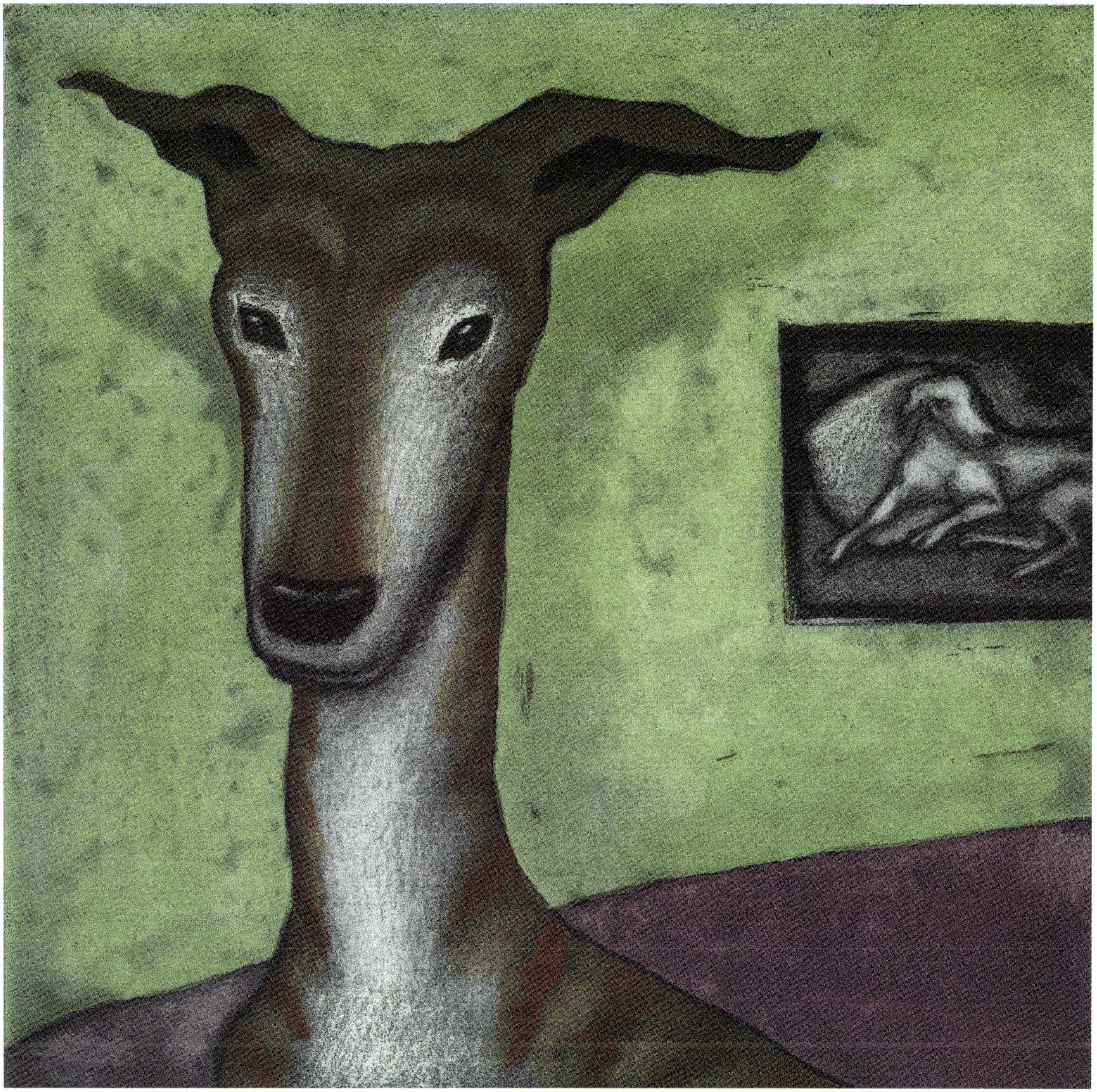

MODIGLIANI'S DOG

Oil on Panel
40 x 40 cm
2005

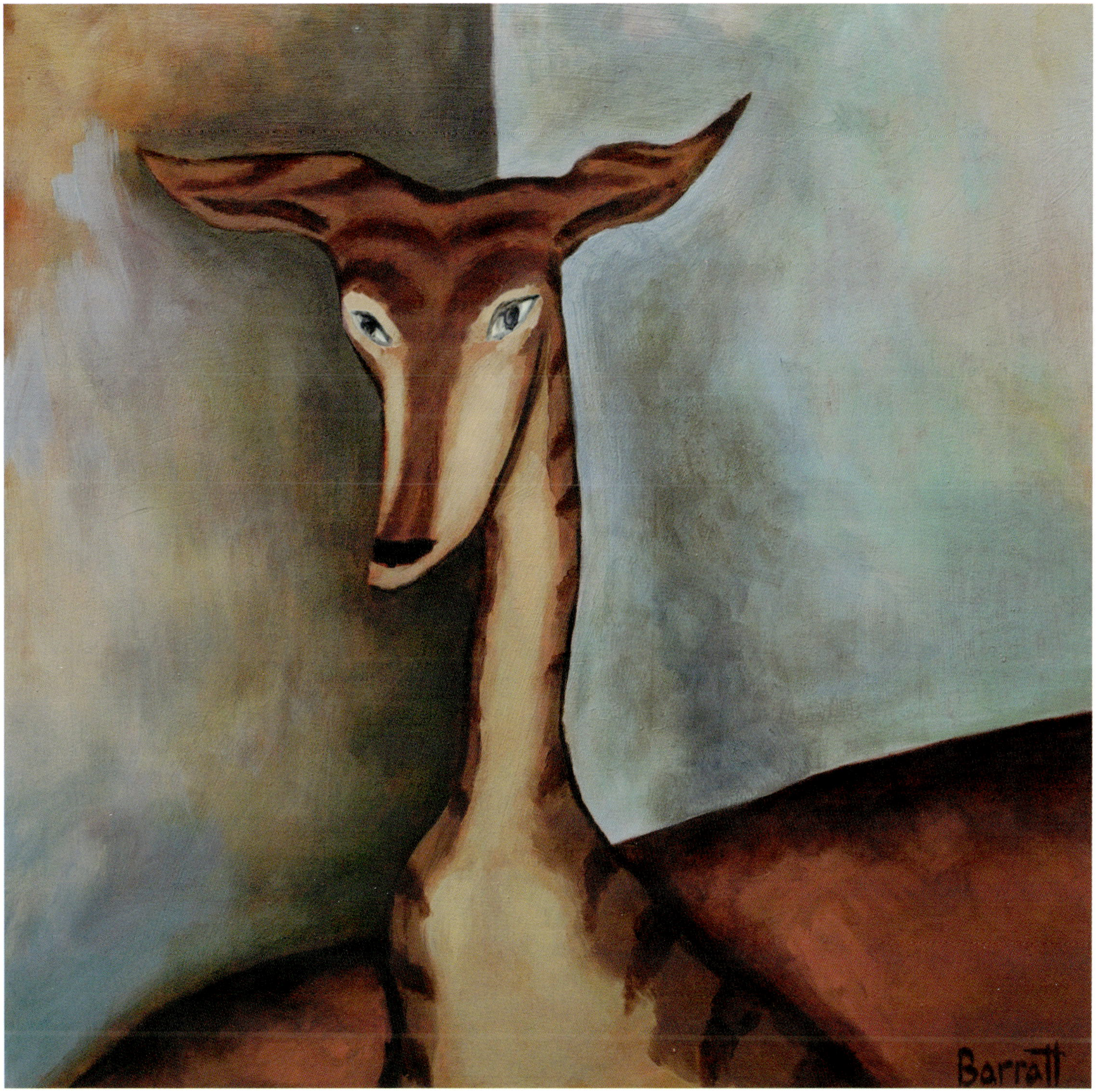
Barratt

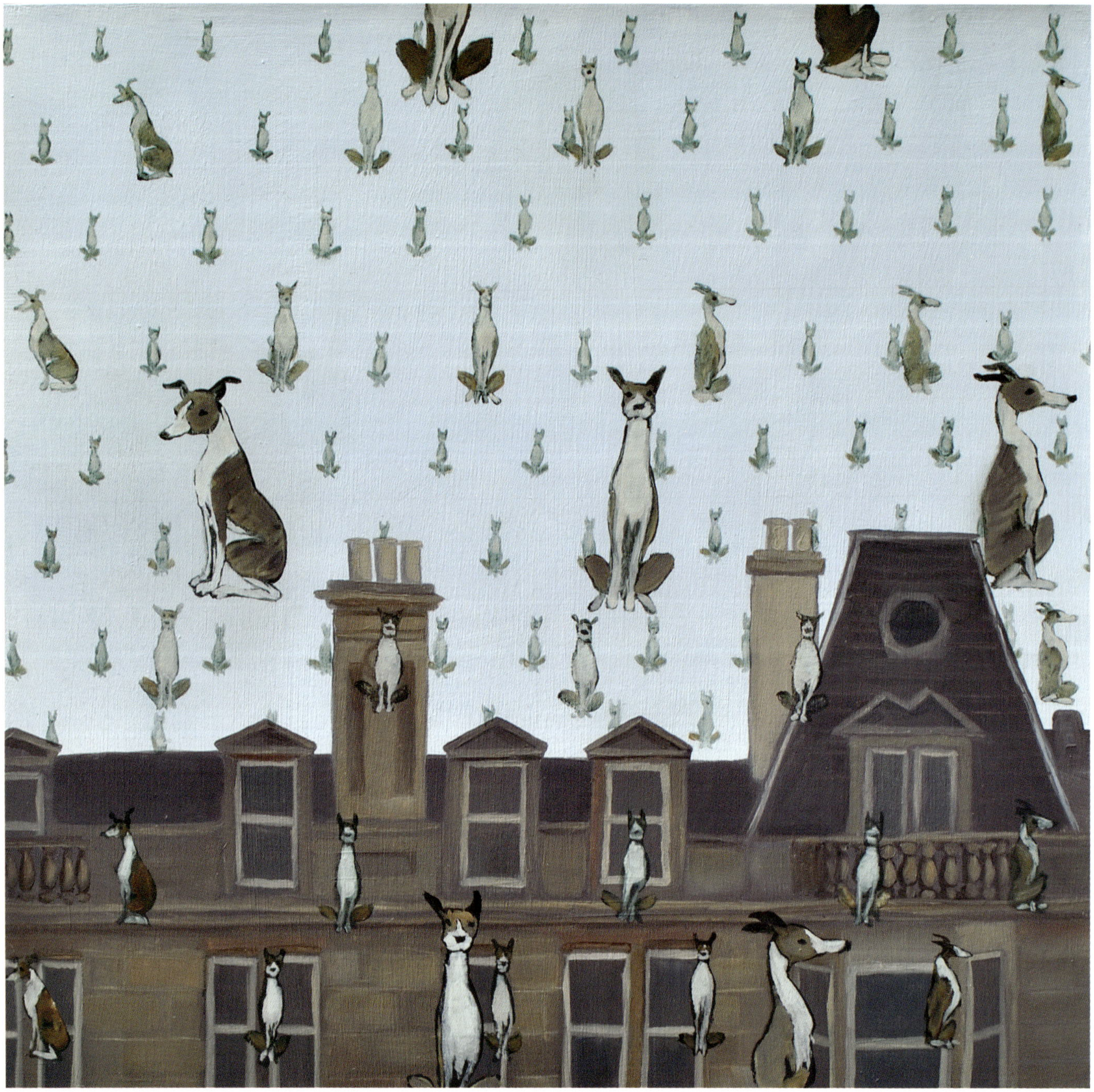

I was commissioned to paint this piece by a woman who cited Magritte as one of her favourite artists. She lived in Glasgow so I based this homage to Magritte's *Giaconda* there. The second version is set near Hyde Park in London.

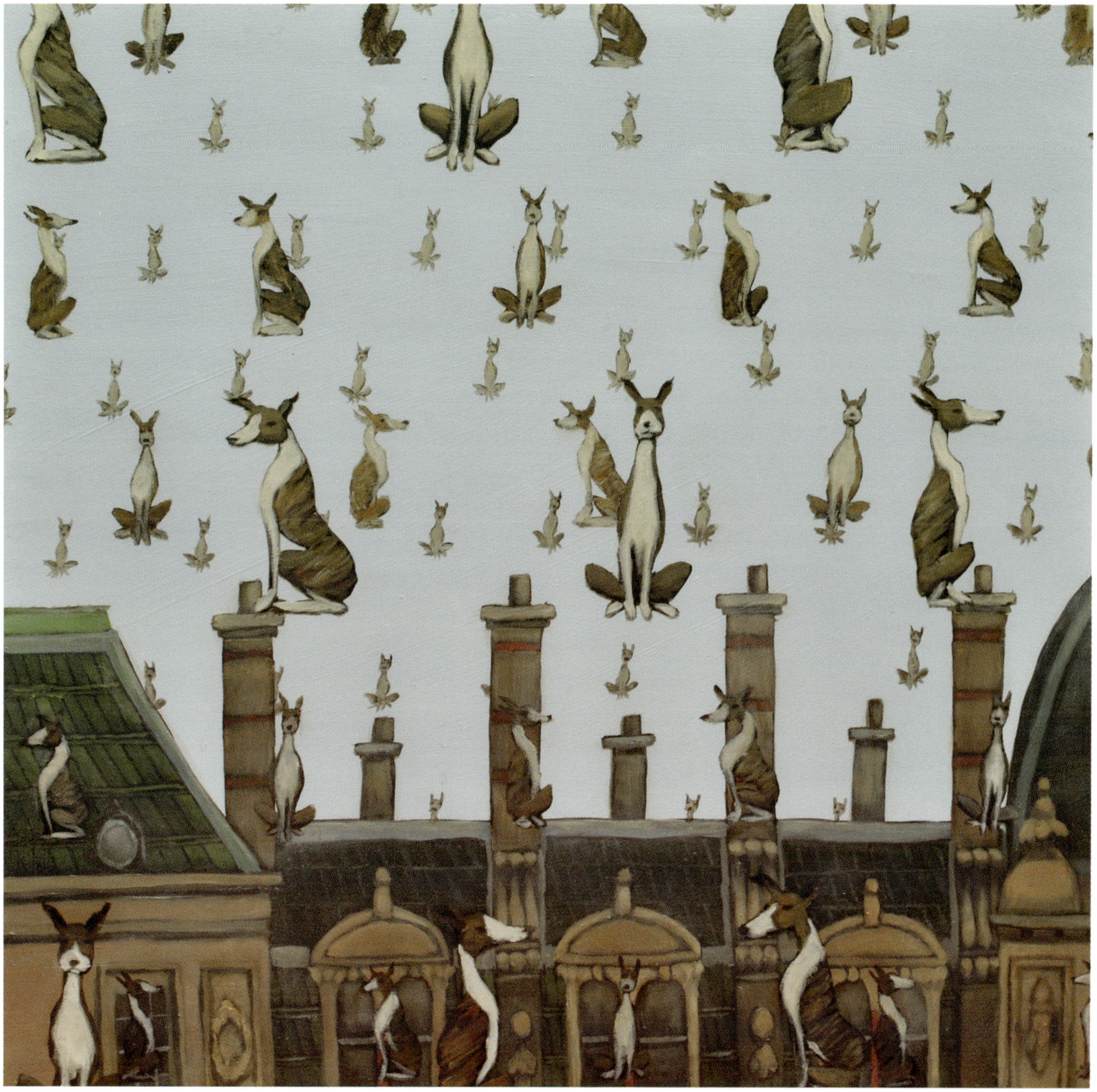

MAGRITTE'S DOGS I AND II

Oil on panel 40 x 40 cm 2010 and 2015

HOLBEIN'S DOG

Oil on panel
40 x 40 cm
2014

This is based on a portrait by Hans Holbein but features an anamorphic dog like the skull in *The Ambassadors.*

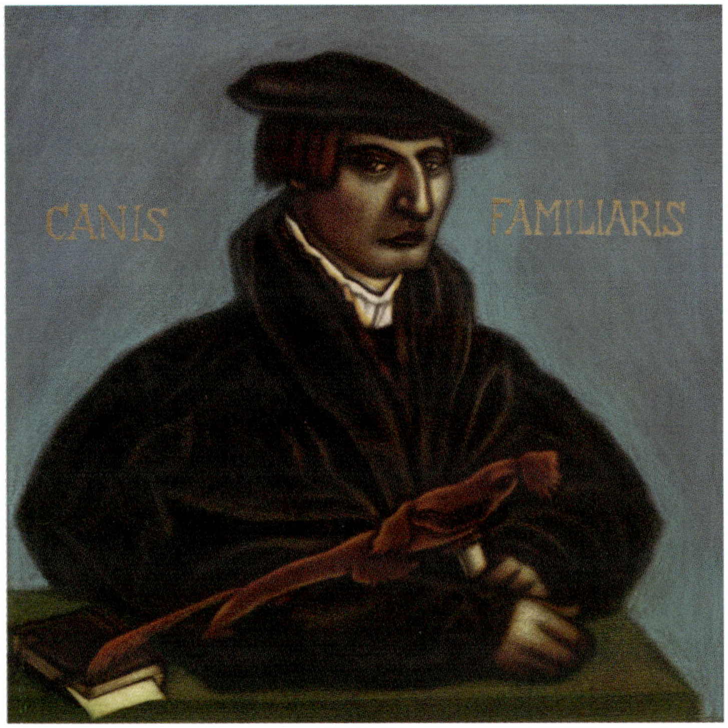

Mezzotint and relief print 22 x 22 cm 2014

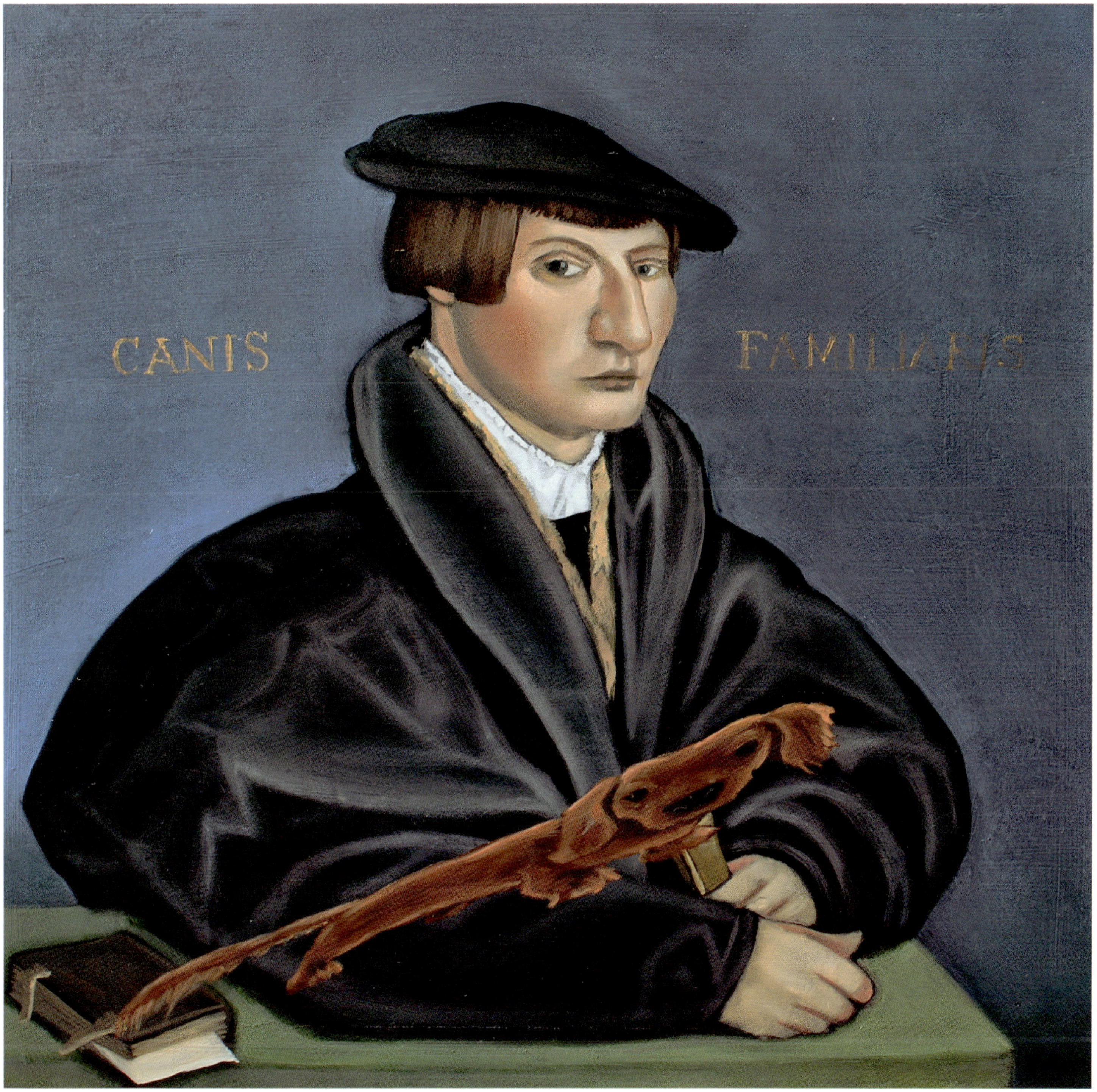
CANIS
FAMILIARIS

DE CHIRICO'S DOG

Oil on panel
40 x 40 cm
2007

Echoing works like *The Charnel House* and *The Mystery and Melancholy of the Street*, I set my nostalgic dedication to Georgio de Chirico in London's King's Cross, which feels like it is gradually disappearing.

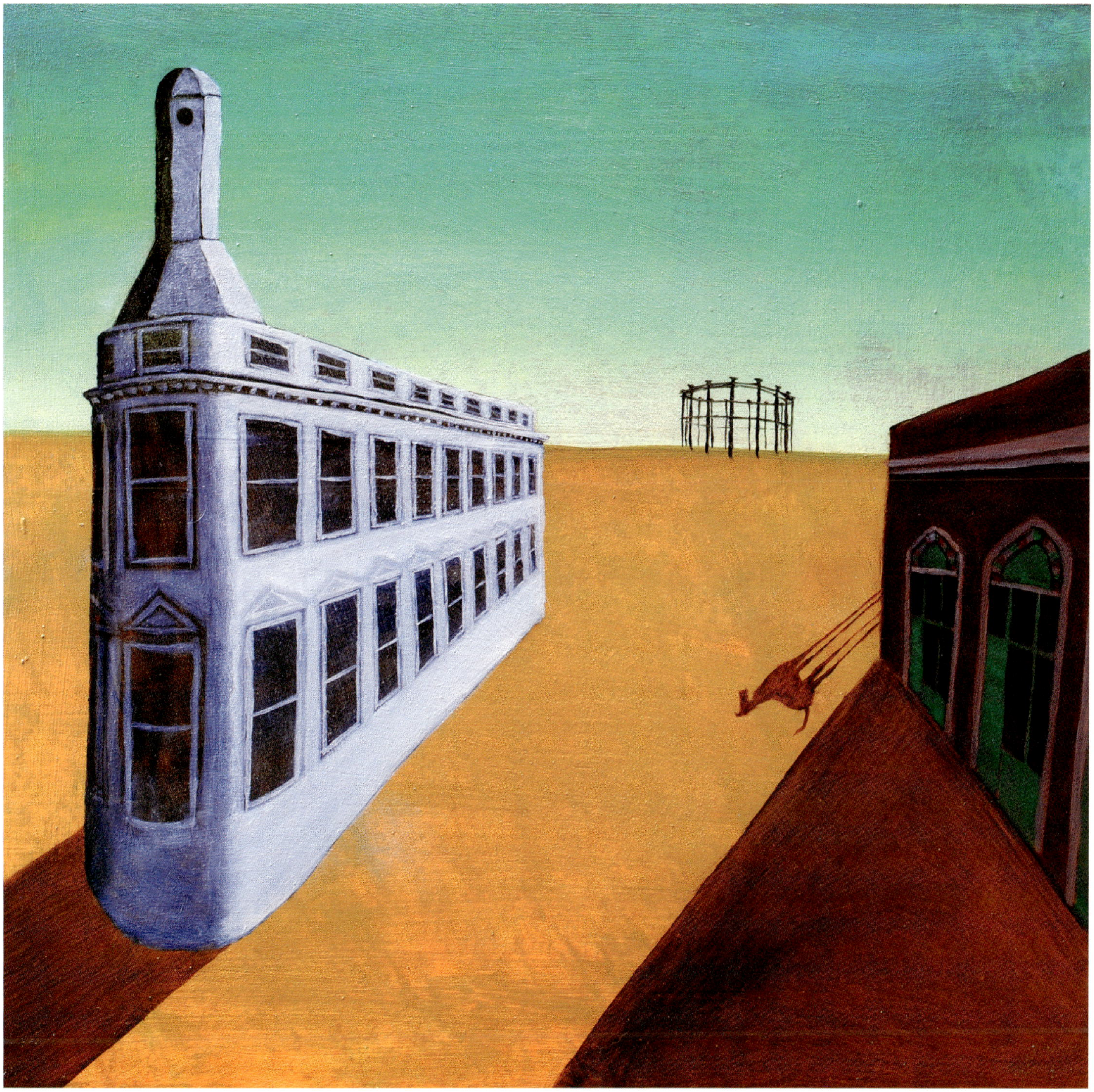

JASPER JOHNS' DOGS

Oil on panel and papier-mâché
40 x 40 cm
2009

Inspired by Jasper Johns' work *Target with Four Faces* at the Museum of Modern Art in New York, the sculptural elements were made of papier-mâché. I was carrying some plasticine with me when I saw a sleeping dog and sculpted these from life. I'm not sure what breed it was – may have been a boxer.

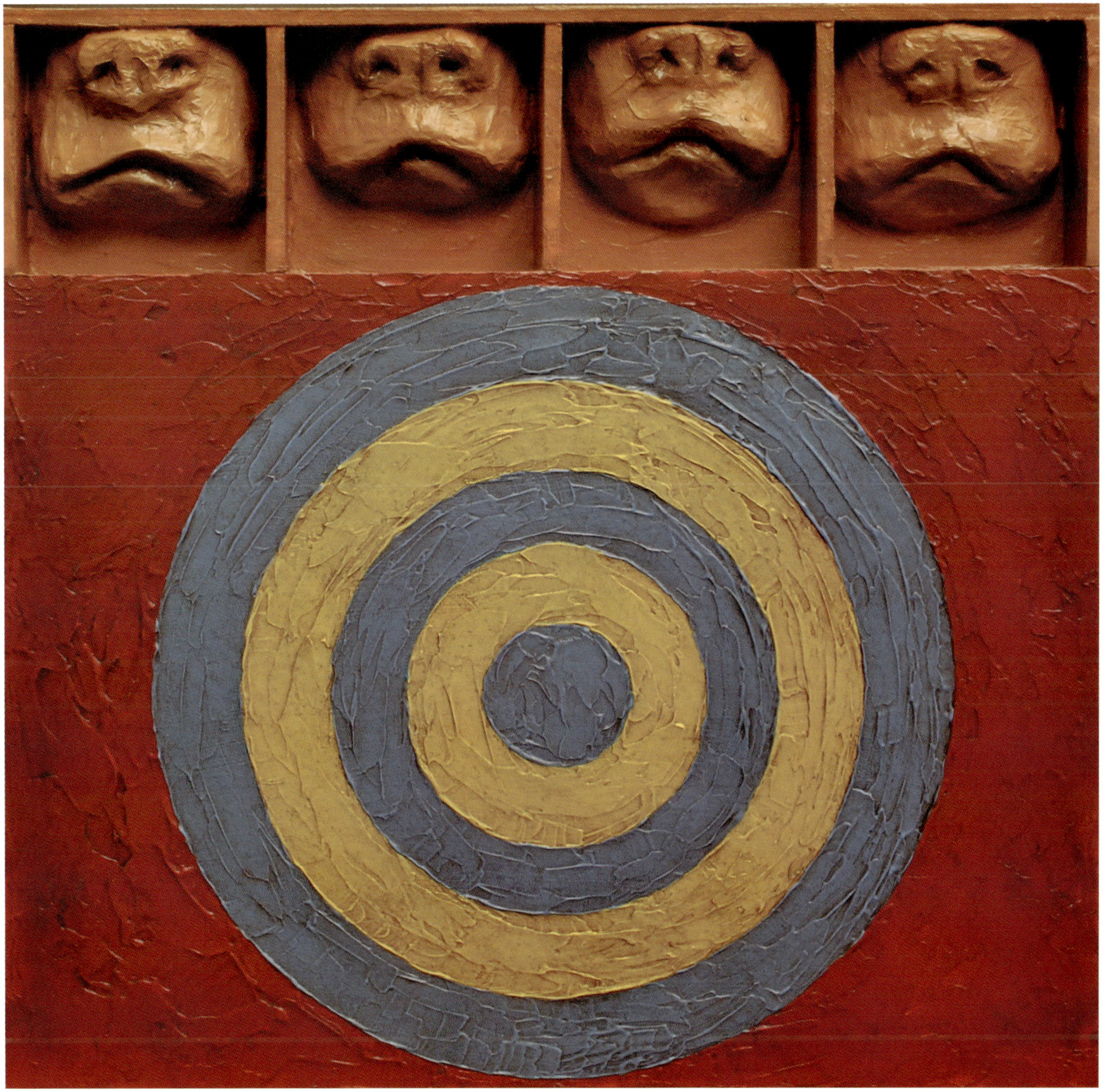

MATISSE'S DOGS

Oil on panel
40 x 40 cm
2015

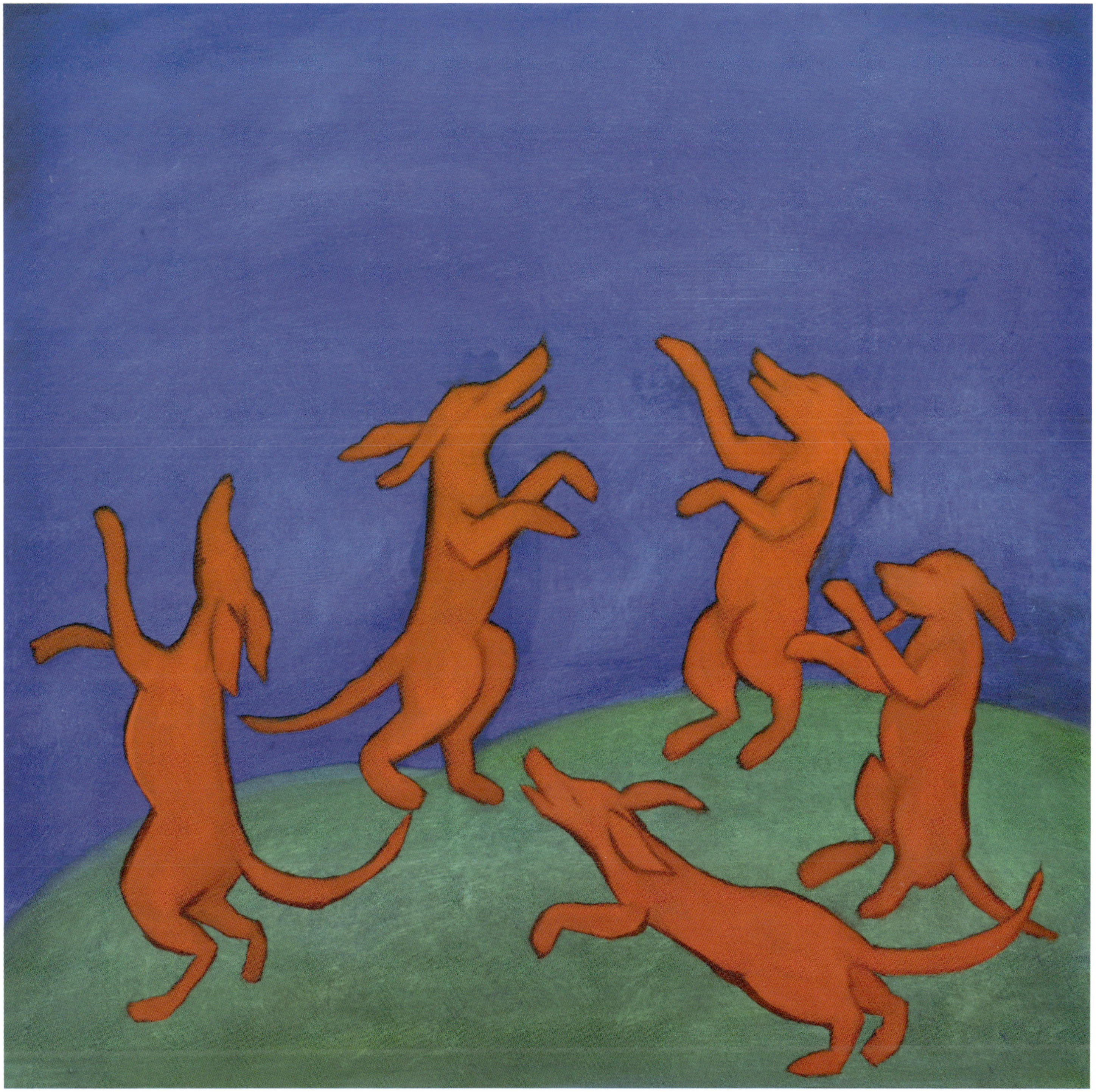

DALI'S DOGS I

Oil on panel
40 x 40 cm
2012

Based on *The Persistence of Memory*, I found the notion of the languid, melting dogs irresistible. The idea to put a cat in the tree came afterwards.

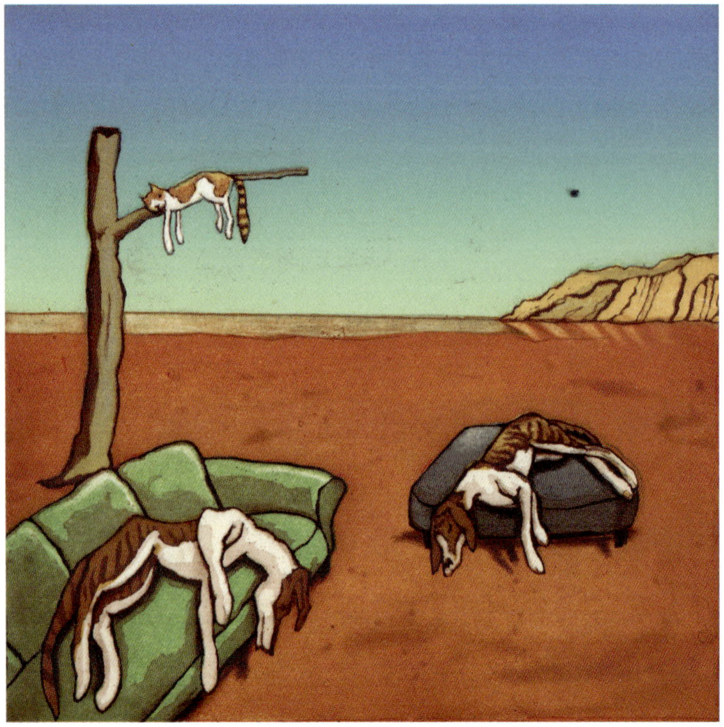

Etching and aquatint 22 x 22 cm 2012

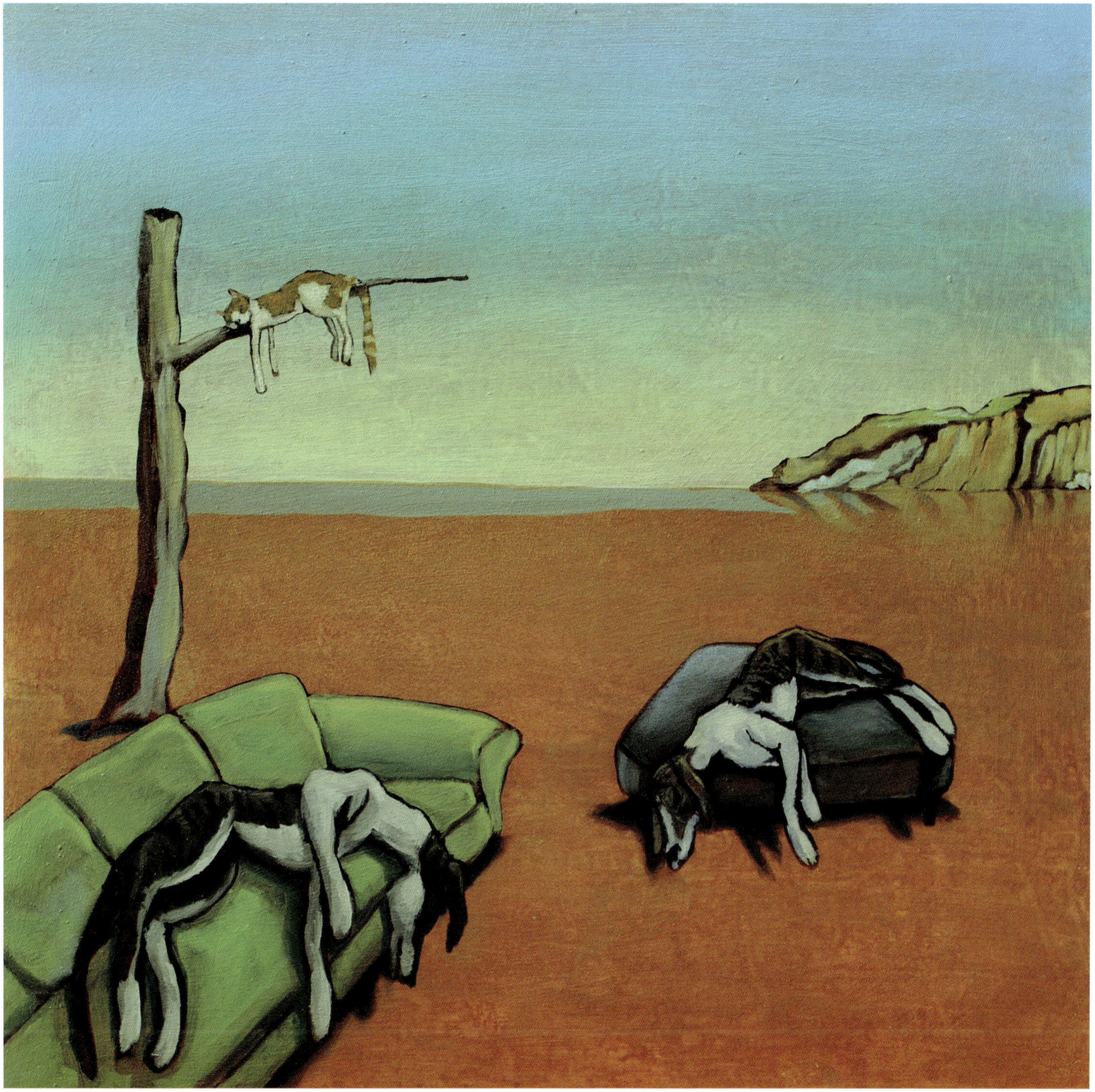

CHRIS OFILI'S DOG

Oil on panel
40 x 40 cm
2009

This piece is a take on Ofili's 1997 work *Blossom.*

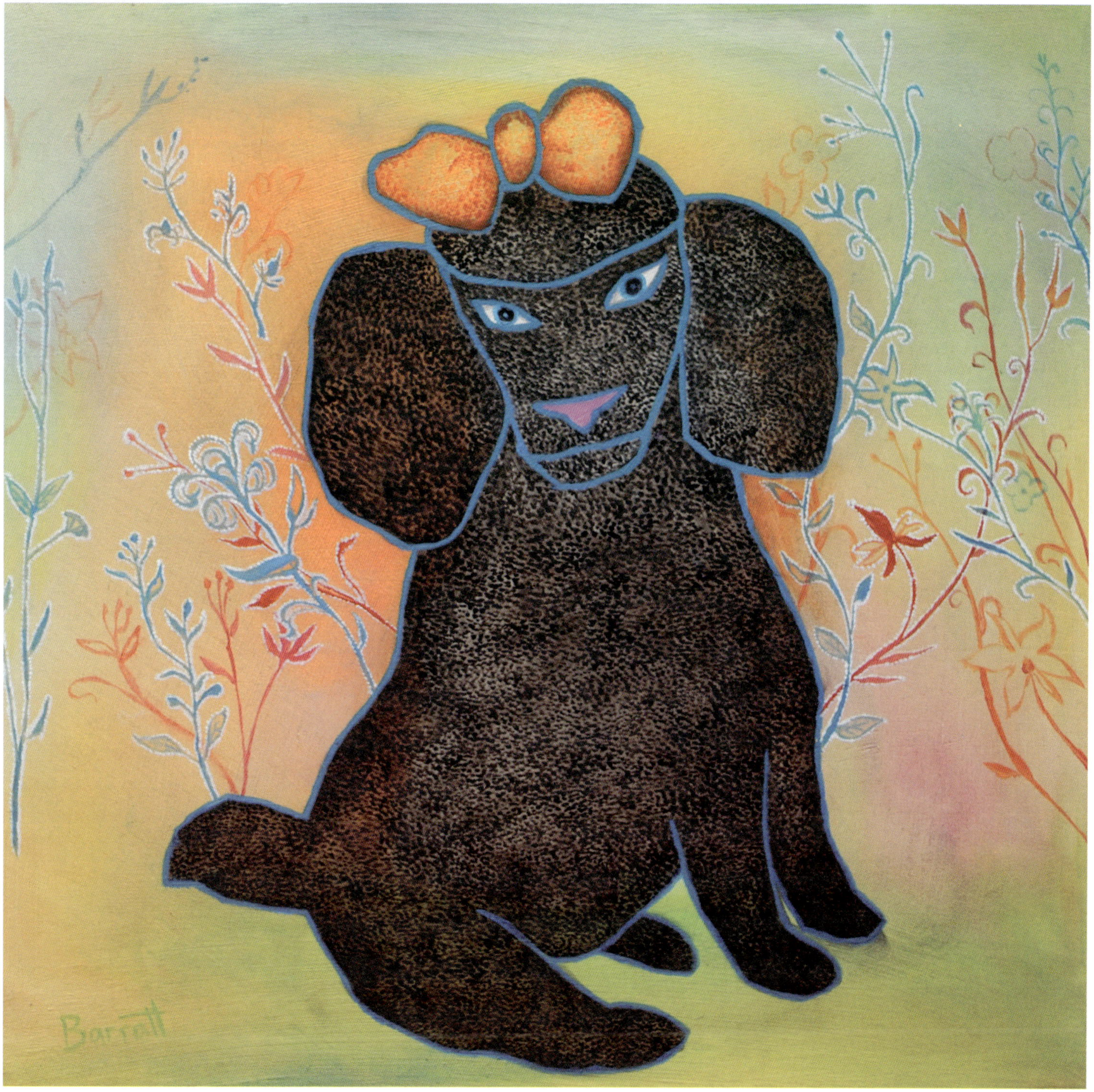
Barratt

CHAGALL'S DOG IN LOVE

Hand-coloured etching and aquatint
22 x 22 cm
2004

The desire to imagine what kind of dog Chagall would have had led to this image which started as an etching but has recurred in many different paintings.

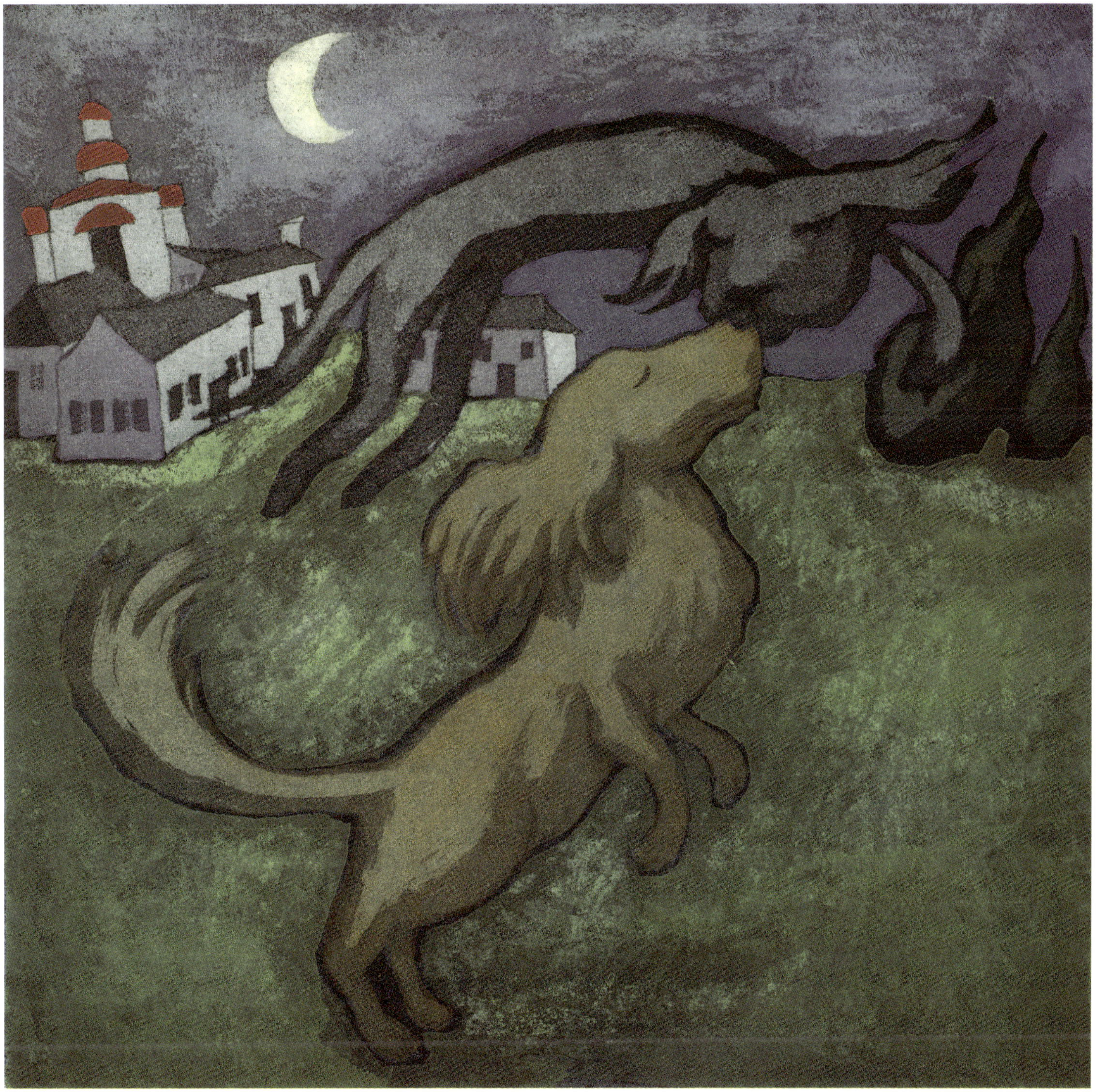

CHAGALL'S DOG IN LOVE I

Oil on panel
40 x 40 cm
2004

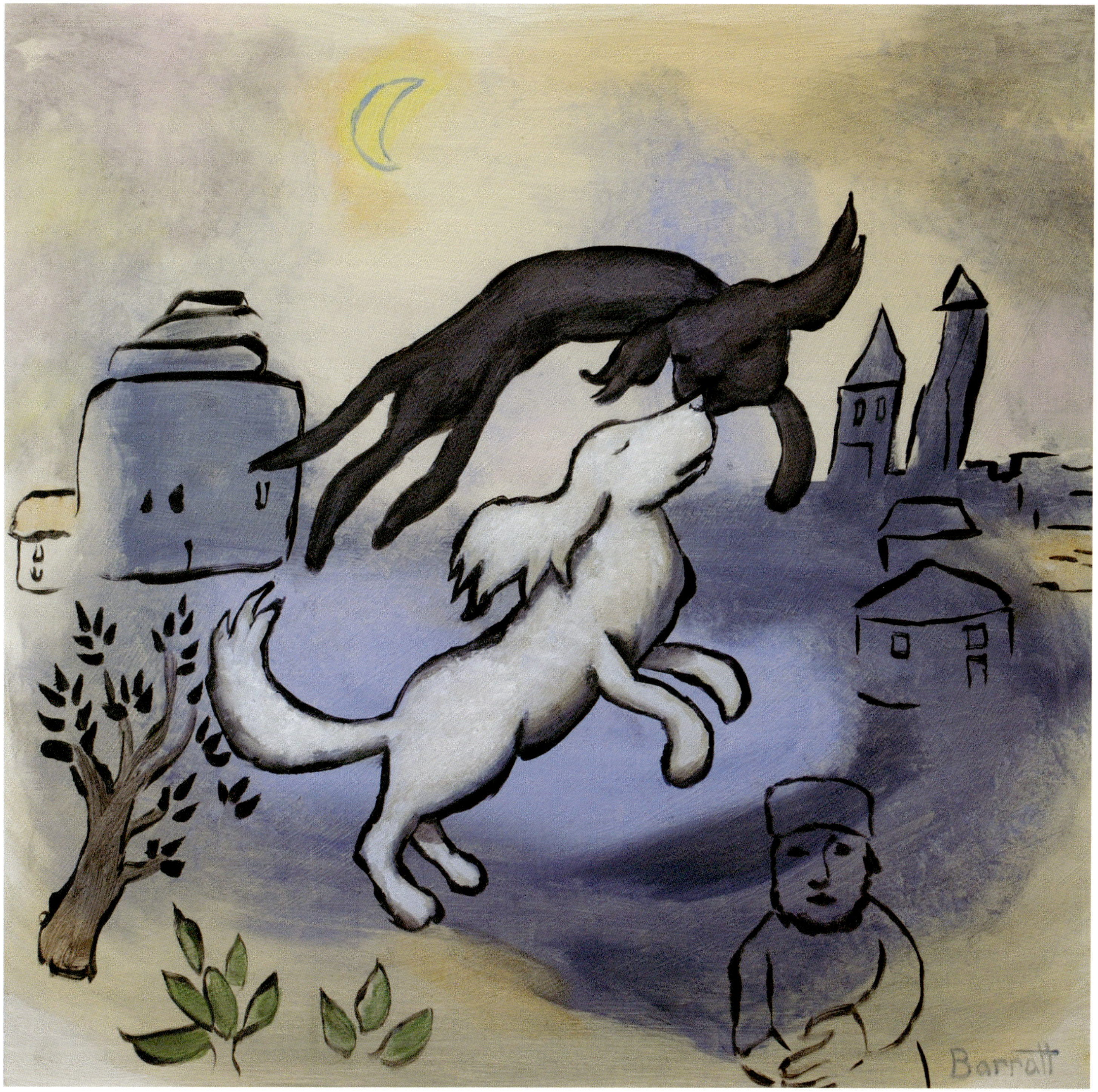
Barratt

CHAGALL'S DOG IN LOVE II

Oil on panel
40 x 40 cm
2013

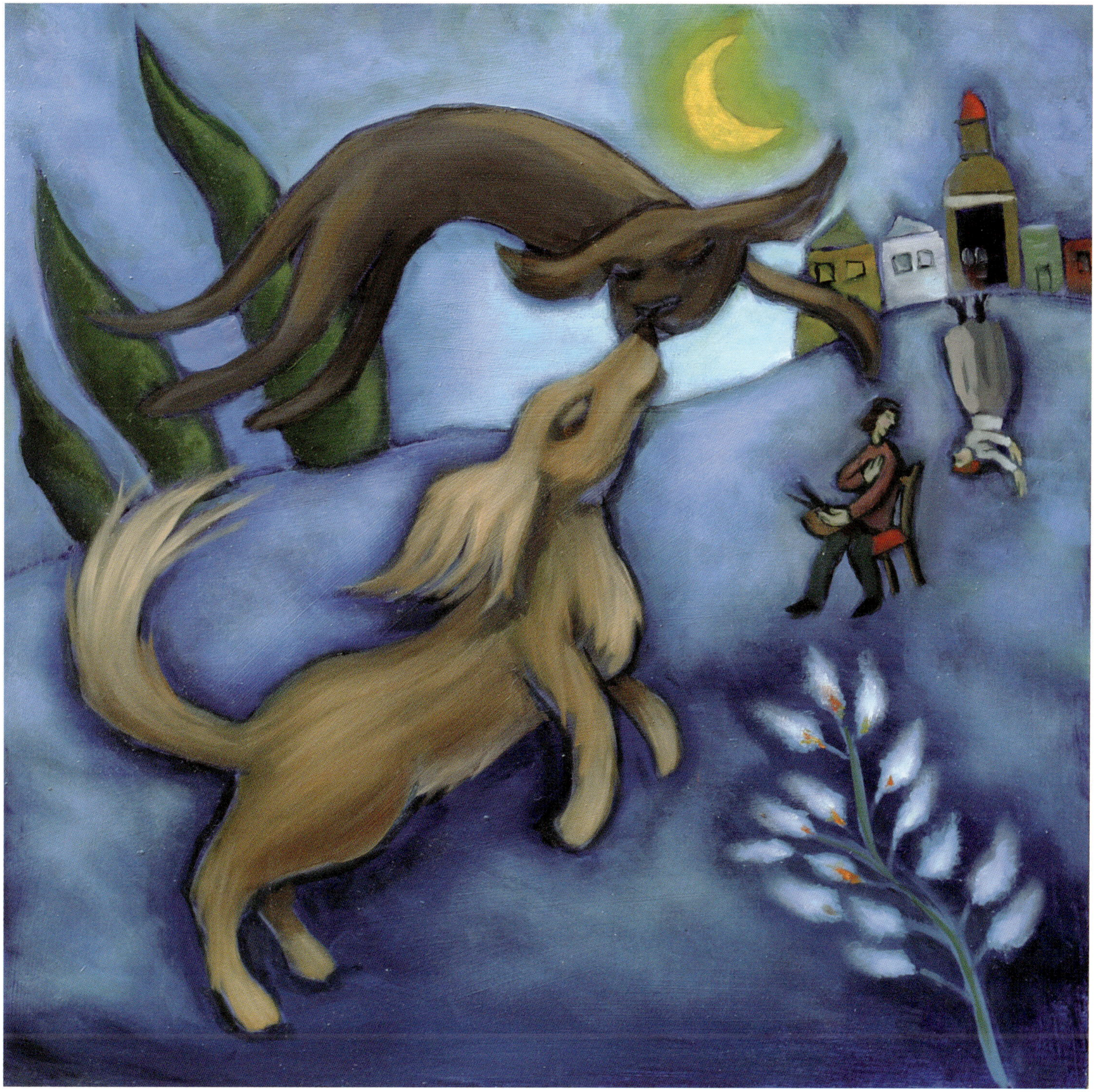

ANTONY GORMLEY'S DOG

Oil on panel
40 x 40 cm
2008

This painting is based on Antony Gormley's sculpture *Domain Field*, a figurative piece which was constructed from small metal bars.

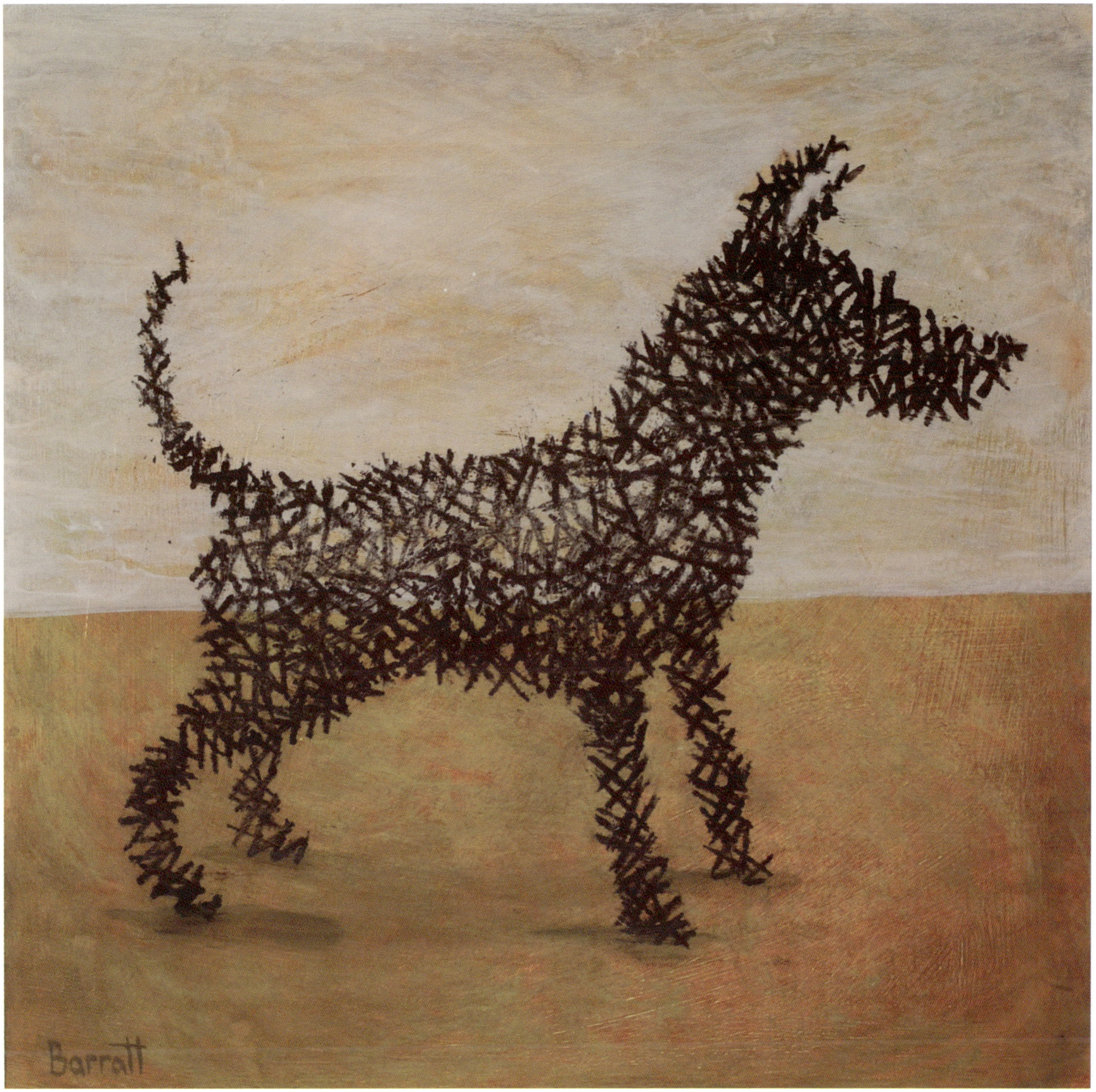
Barratt

BRIDGET RILEY'S DOG

Screenprint
22 x 22 cm
2015

Screenprinting was the logical technique for this homage to Bridget Riley's 1960's optical paintings.

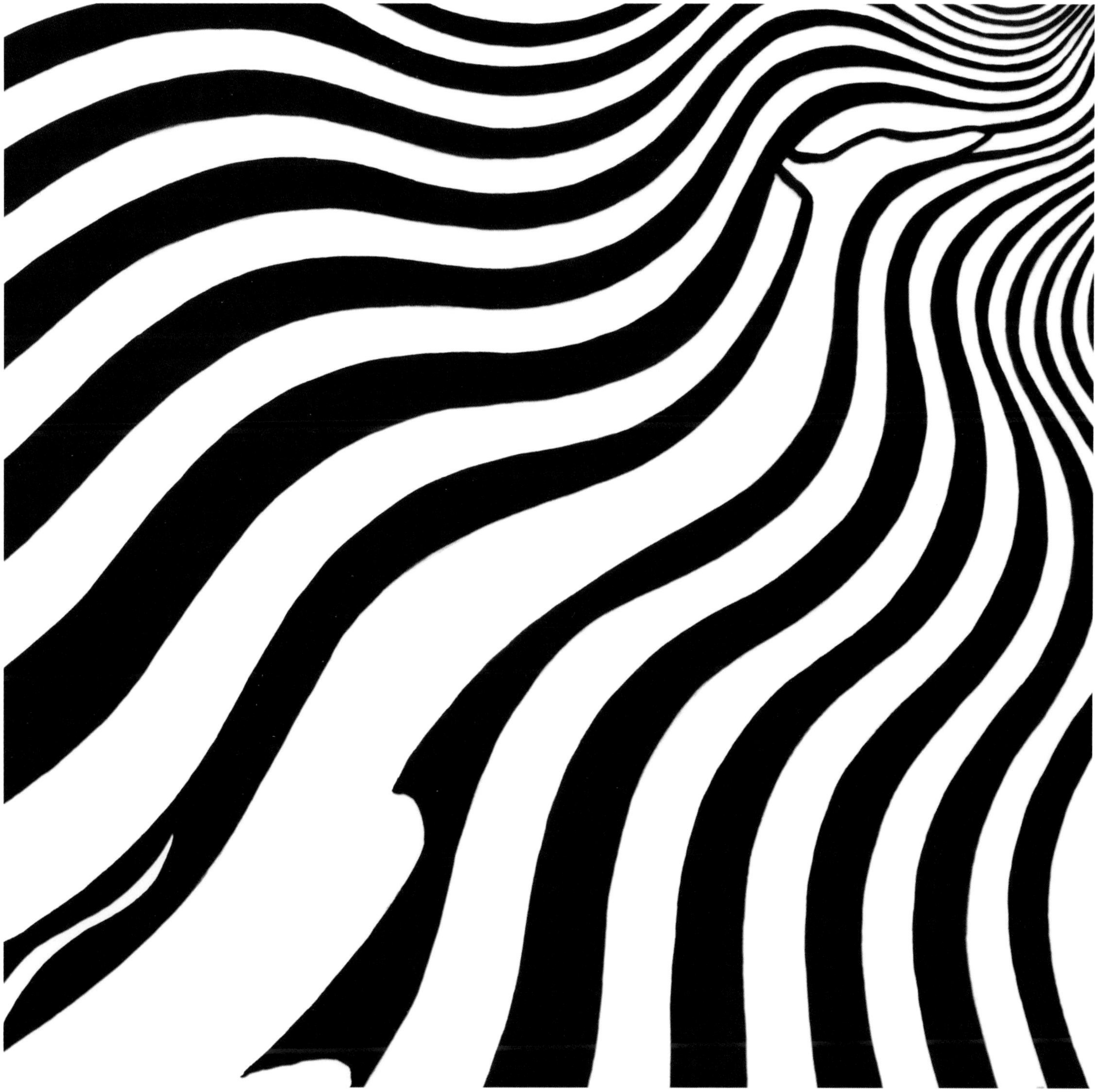

DALI'S DOGS II

Oil on panel
40 x 40 cm
2015

A friend referred to having seen Salvador Dali's *Temptation of Saint Anthony* and this image popped into my head fully formed.

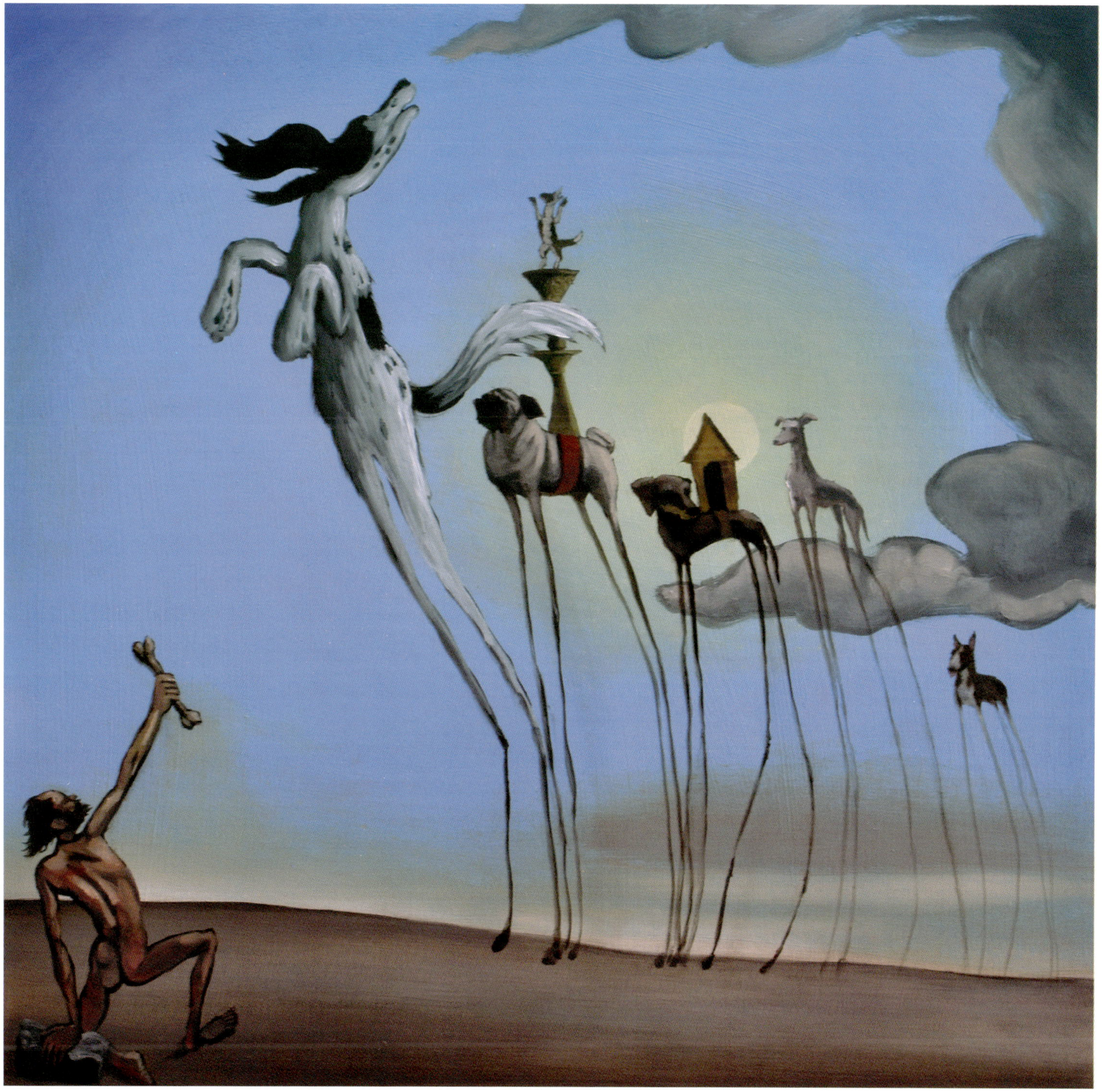

REMBRANDT'S DOG

Etching on tea-stained
Japanese gampi chine-collé
22 x 22 cm 2014

This etching was another piece like the Chagall that started from an attempt to picture what kind of a dog Rembrandt would have had. It is printed on the Japanese gampi paper that was favoured by Rembrandt.

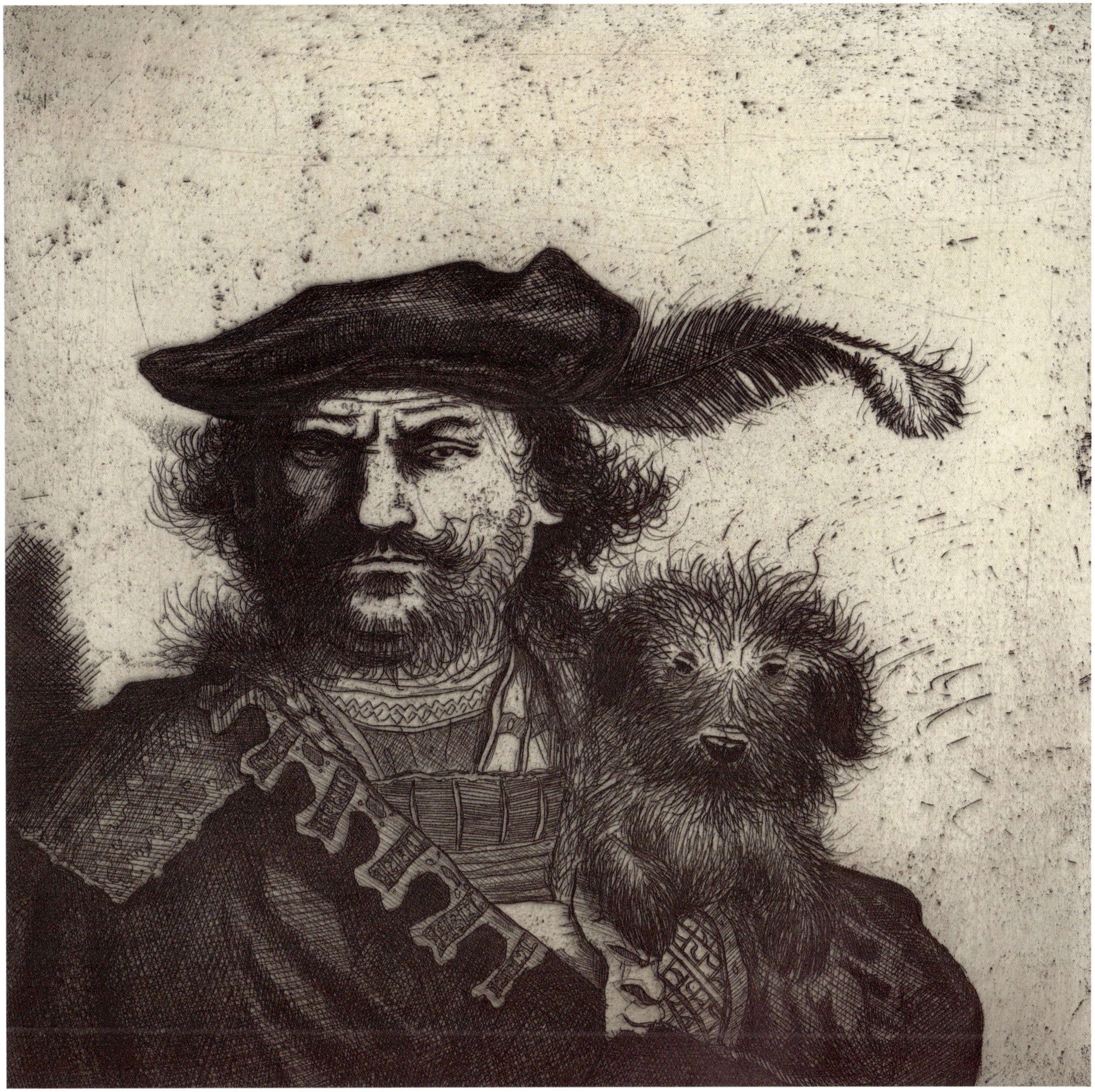

DE KOONING'S DOG

Lithograph
22 x 22 cm
2014

This is based on Robert Rauschenberg's piece *Erased de Kooning* where he obtained and then erased a drawing by fellow artist Willem de Kooning. Realising that the idea wouldn't work if I was as thorough in my erasing, I did many attempts at this before I was happy with how much drawing should be left.

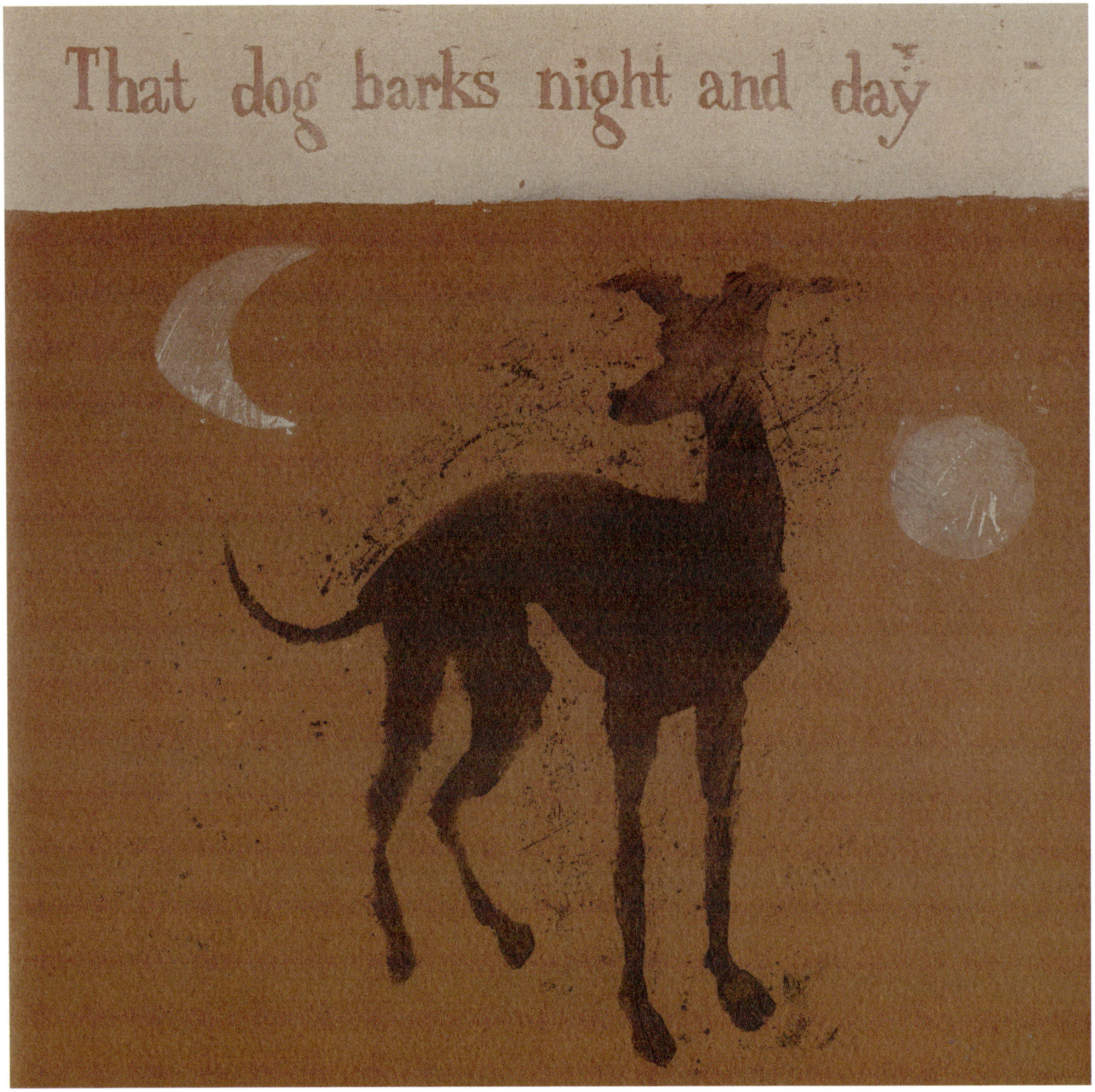

The ideas behind *Cole Porter's Dog I* and *II* were given to me by my friend Fred. I tried various techniques to realise these until I came up with a simple treatment that allowed the ideas to shine.

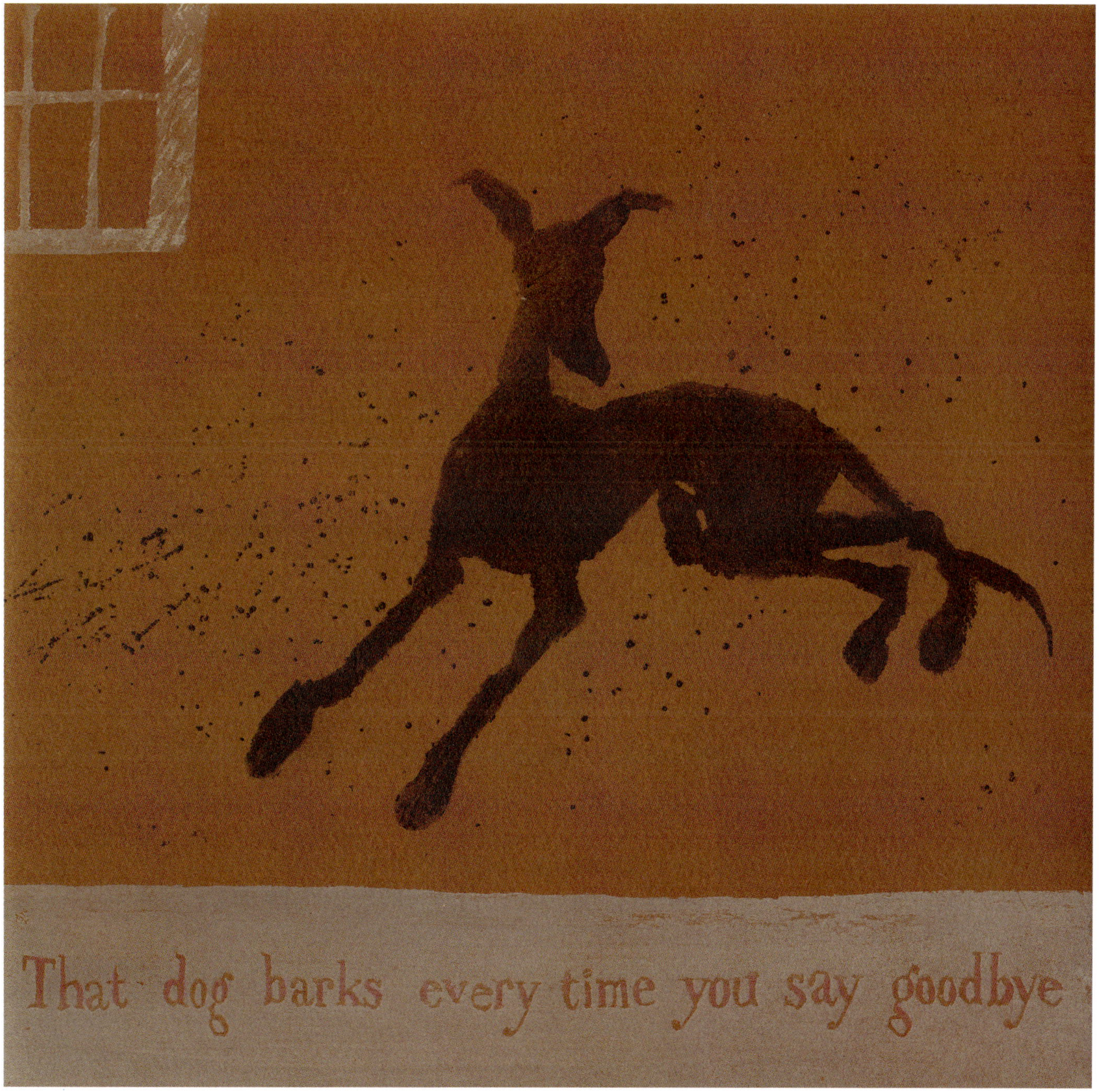

COLE PORTER'S DOG I AND II

Etching and aquatint on chine-collé 22 x 22 cm 2012

PICASSO'S CAT

Oil on panel
40 x 40 cm
2014

A loving dedication to Picasso's 1901 painting *Child with a Dove* that I saw many times before it left Britain to a private collection.

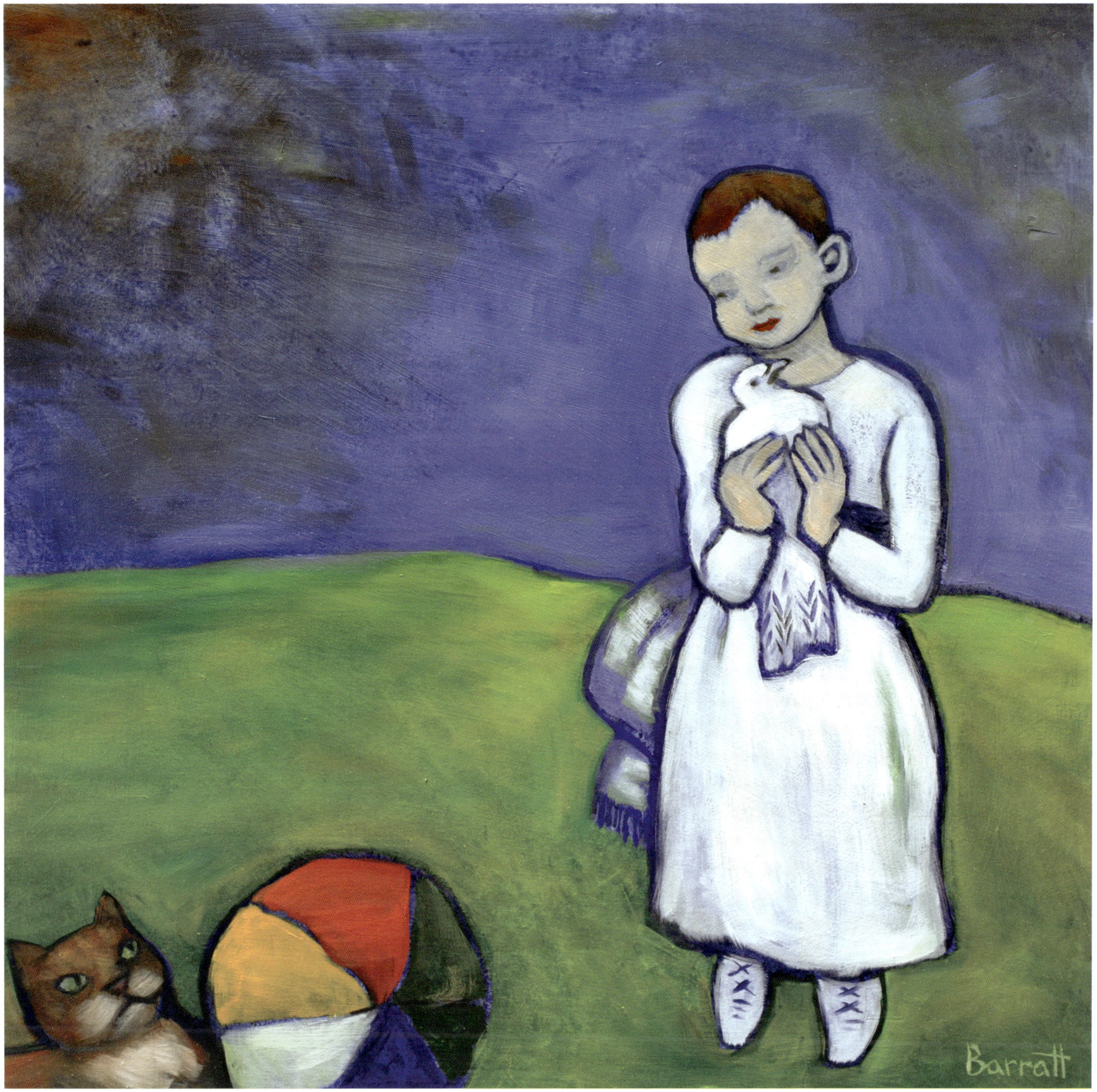
Barratt

EDWARD HOPPER'S DOG

Etching and aquatint
22 x 22 cm
2012

Another homage to one of my favourite paintings, this time Edward Hopper's iconic *Nighthawks*.

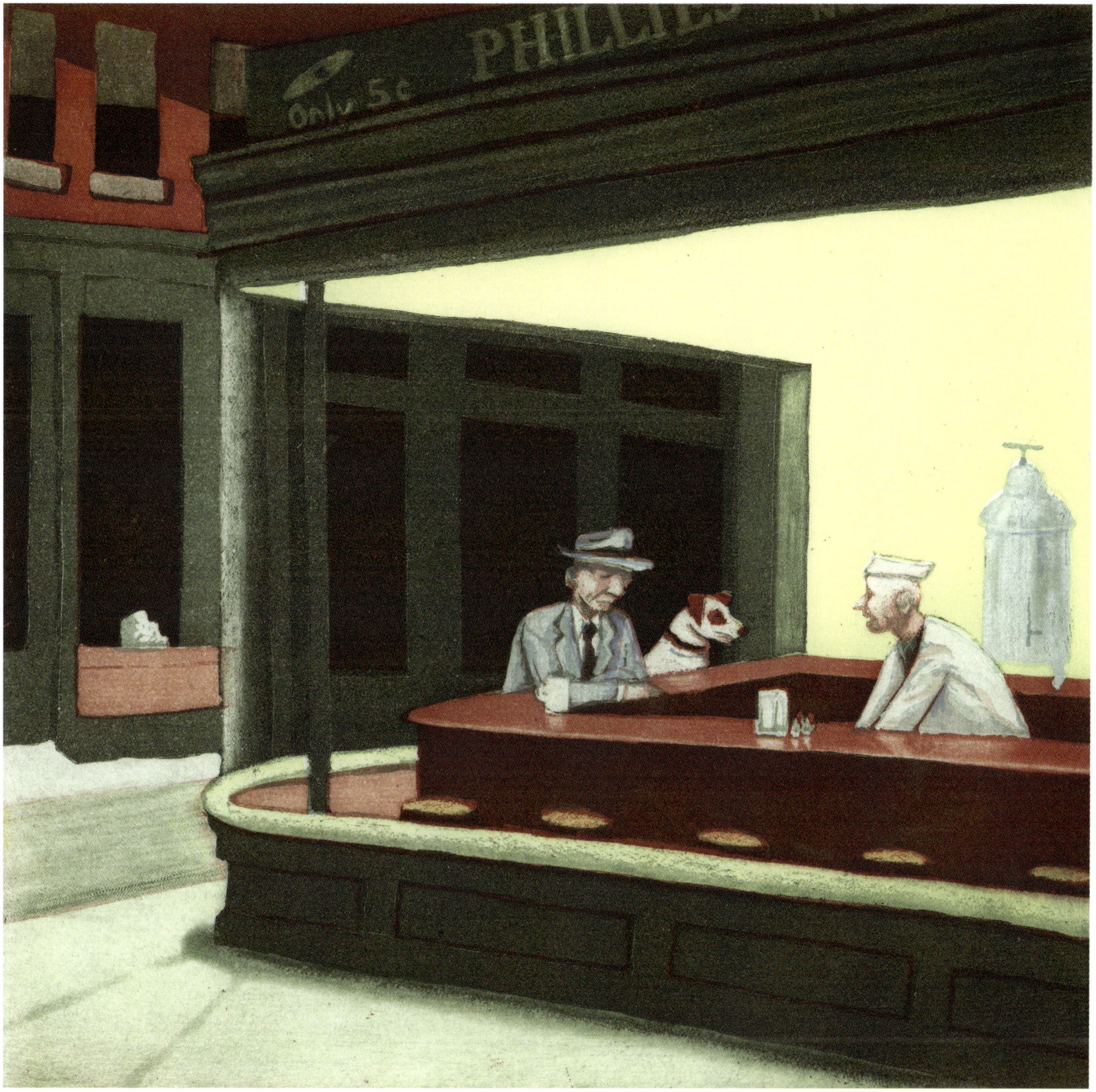
PHILLIES
Only 5¢

ANDY WARHOL'S DOG

Etching and woodcut on chine-collé
22 x 22 cm
2010

I saw a repeated image of a dog food tin as the perfect interpretation of Warhol's *Campbell Soup* screenprints and created the image by combining an etching on chine-collé with a woodcut. I'm often criticised in London for having chosen to depict an American 1960s dog food but I still believe that it was the right decision.

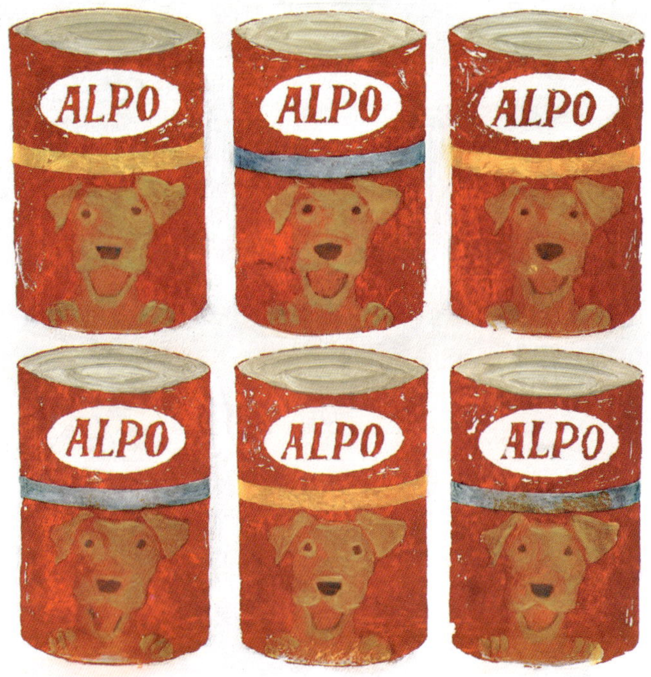

Oil on panel 40 x 40 cm 2010

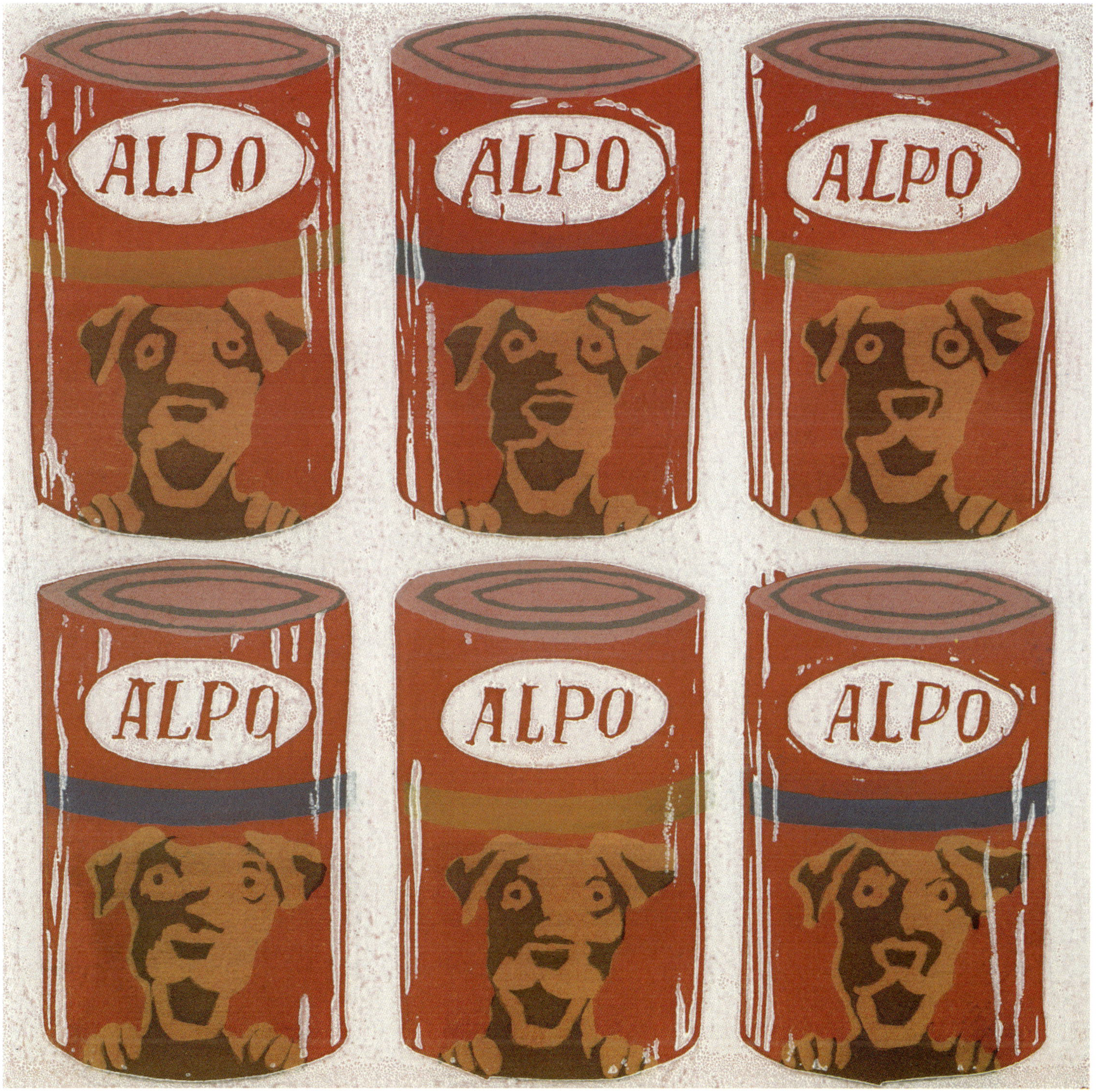
ALPO
ALPO
ALPO
ALPO
ALPO
ALPO

DUBUFFET'S DOG

Oil on panel
40 x 40 cm
2008

This painting is a direct take on *The Cow with the Subtle Nose* (great title!) and had various layers of paint before the subject started to emerge.

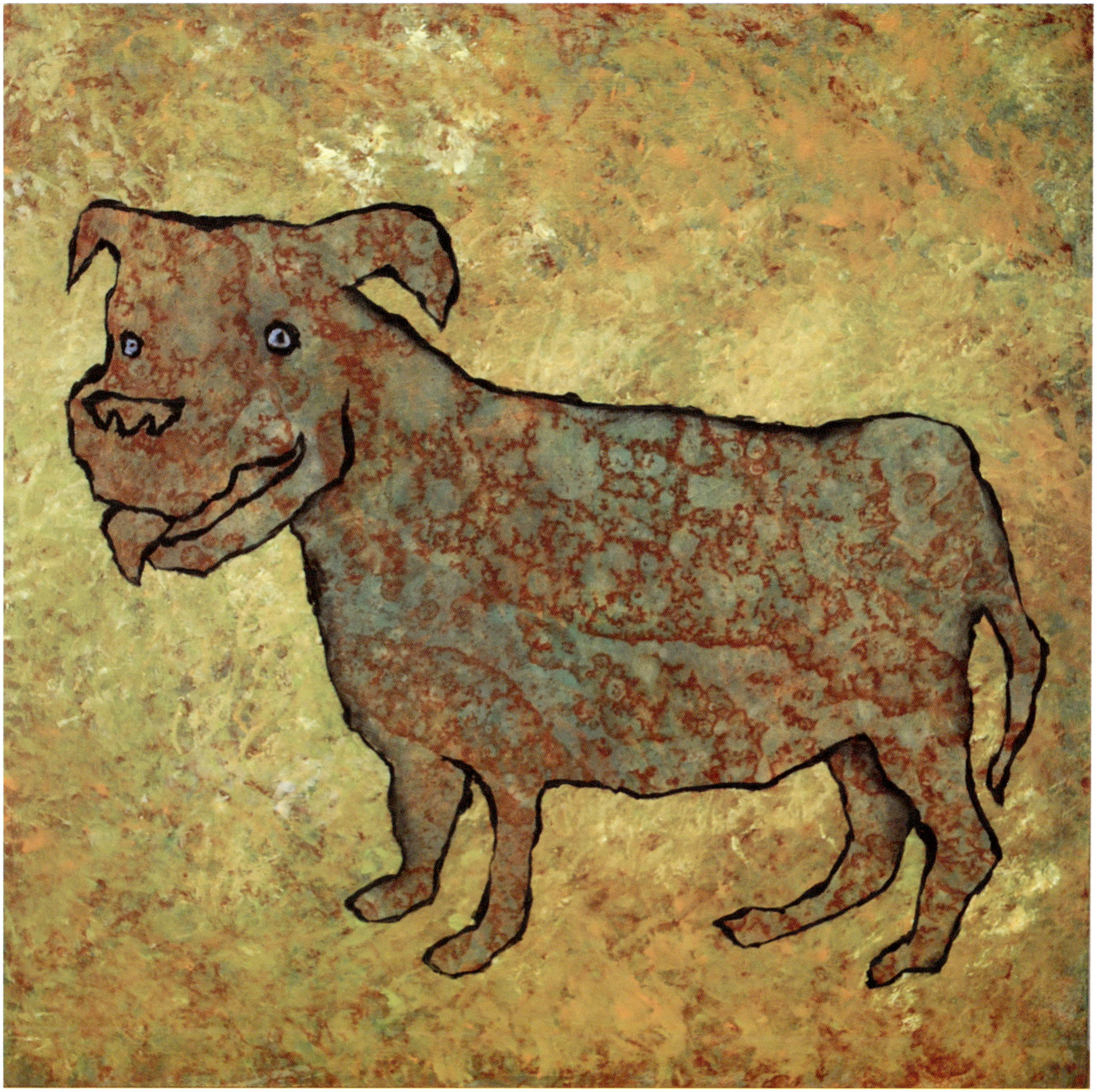

ANTONY GORMLEY'S DOGS

Etching and aquatint
22 x 22 cm
2010

Antony Gormley's sculpture *The Field* has always been one of my favourite works. My two daughters and I made about sixty dogs out of clay and this piece is a photo etching comprised of photographs of various groupings of those sculptures. Although the mission had been to sculpt dogs, my youngest daughter also made a monkey and a hippo. I liked the monkey so much I included it.

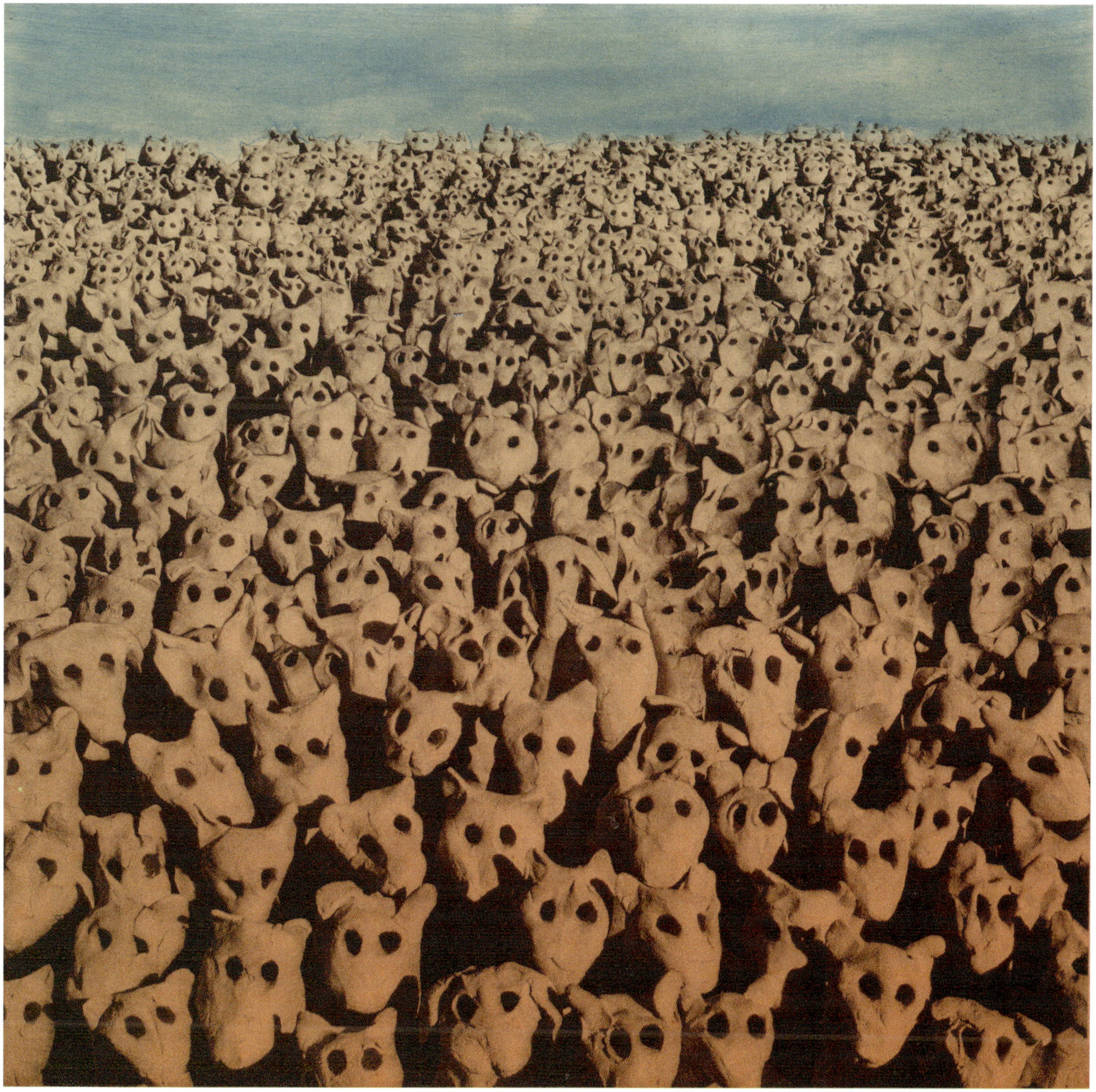

REMBRANDT'S DOG

Oil on panel
40 x 40 cm
2015

This was the result of another commission where I was asked to do a painted version of my etching *Rembrandt's dog*.

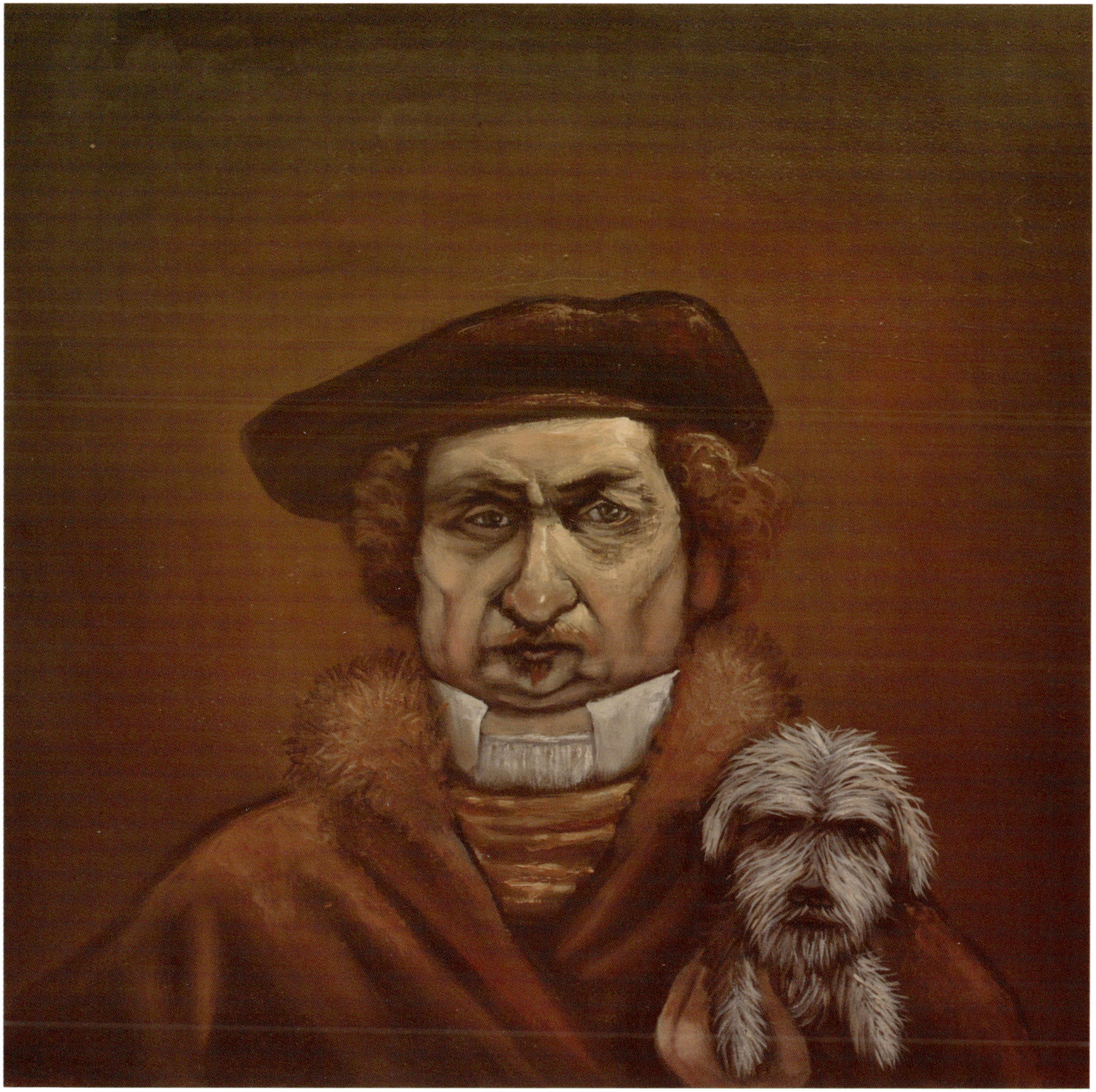

HOCKNEY'S DOG

Oil on panel
40 x 40 cm
2015

This piece was inspired during one of my trips to see *A Bigger Picture*, David Hockney's impressive one-man show at the Royal Academy. It is one of a handful of pieces to include a portrait of the artist.

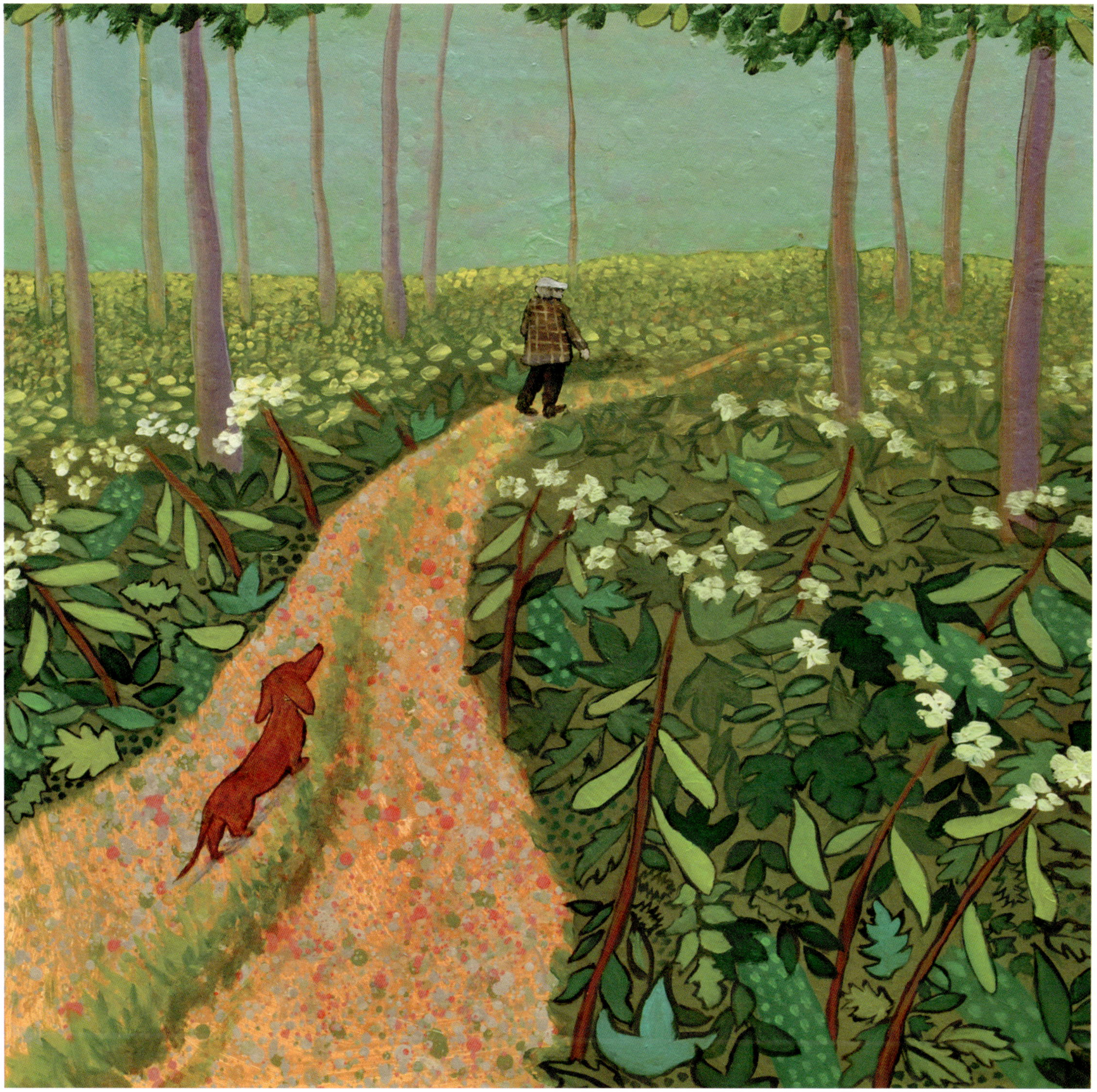

ROUSSEAU'S CAT

Oil on panel
40 x 40 cm
2007

Based on Rousseau's *The Gypsy* that hangs in the Museum of Modern Art in New York. As with the cats of Van Gogh, Yves Klein and Matisse this was inspired by my cat. This time from the way she stands on my chest every morning staring at my face.

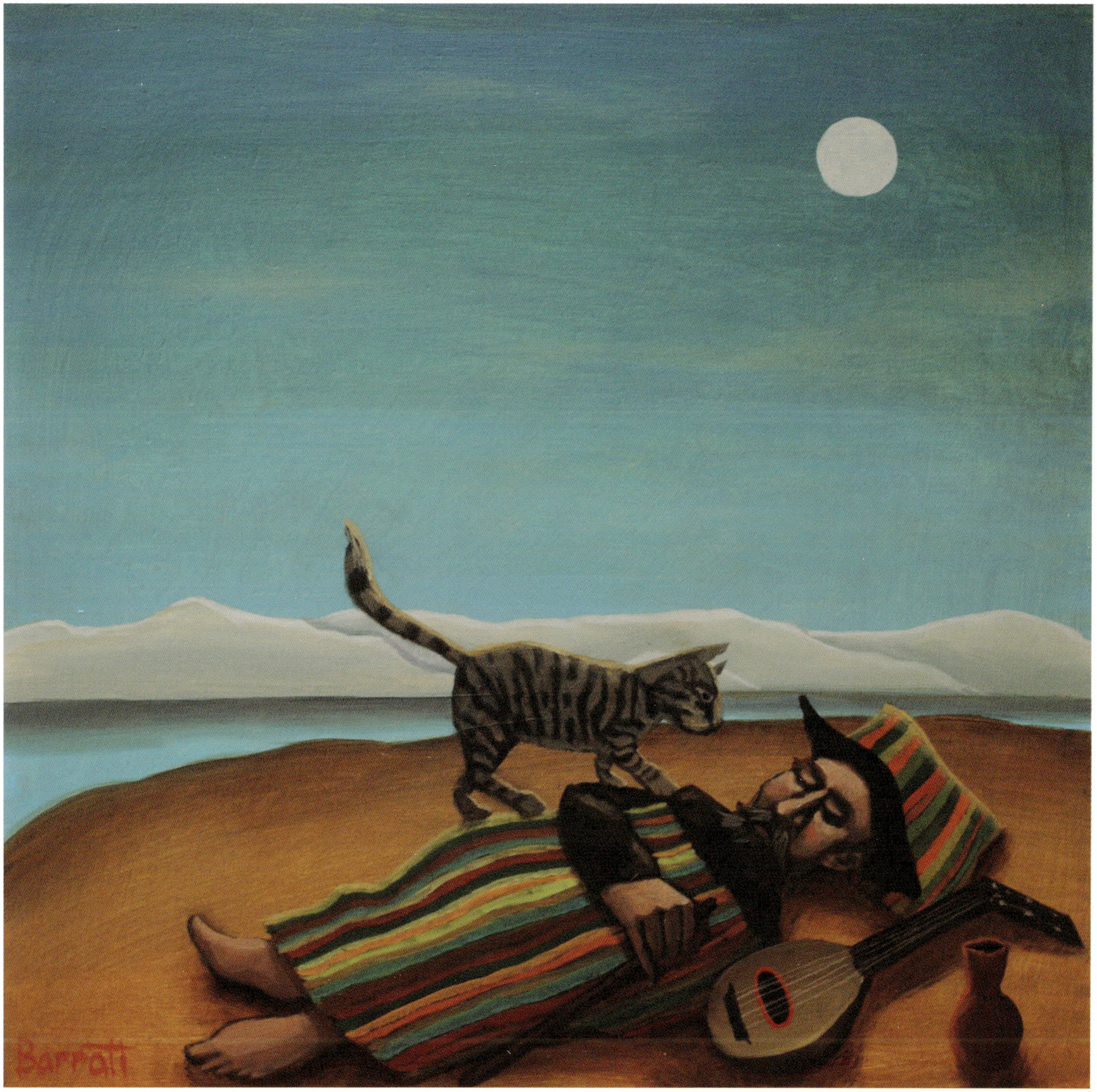
Barratt

LICHTENSTEIN'S DOG

Etching and aquatint
22 x 22 cm
2010

This image was taken from a detail lifted from a 1960's comic book featuring a conversation between Superman and his dog Krypto.
I removed the entire dialogue except for Krypto's final enthusiastic response.

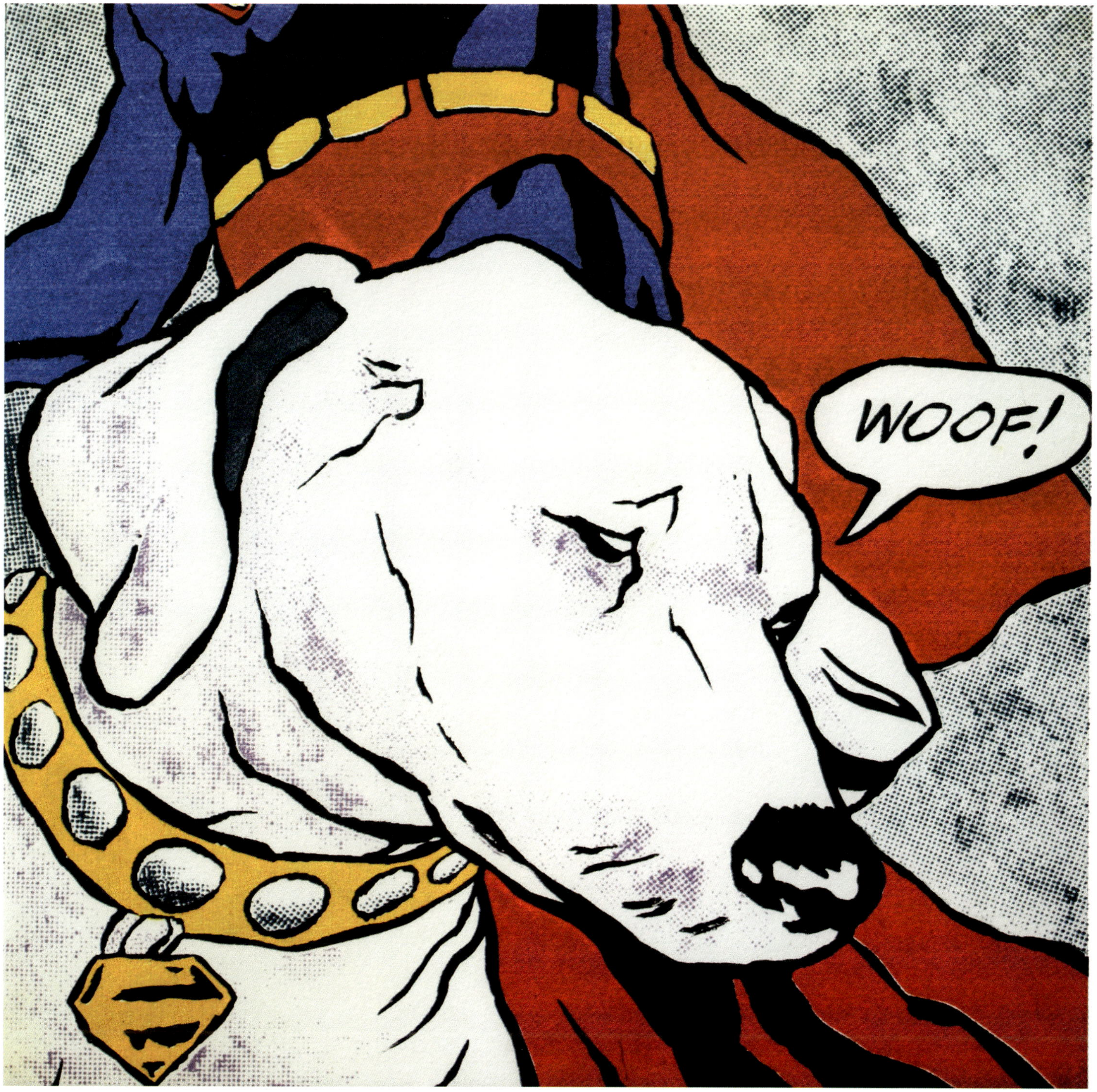
WOOF!

JACKSON POLLOCK'S DOG

Aquatint
22 x 22 cm
2009

The success of this piece all comes from imagining the moment when Pollock realises his error. From biographies I have read I suspect that he would have tried to salvage the painting before cleaning the poor dog.

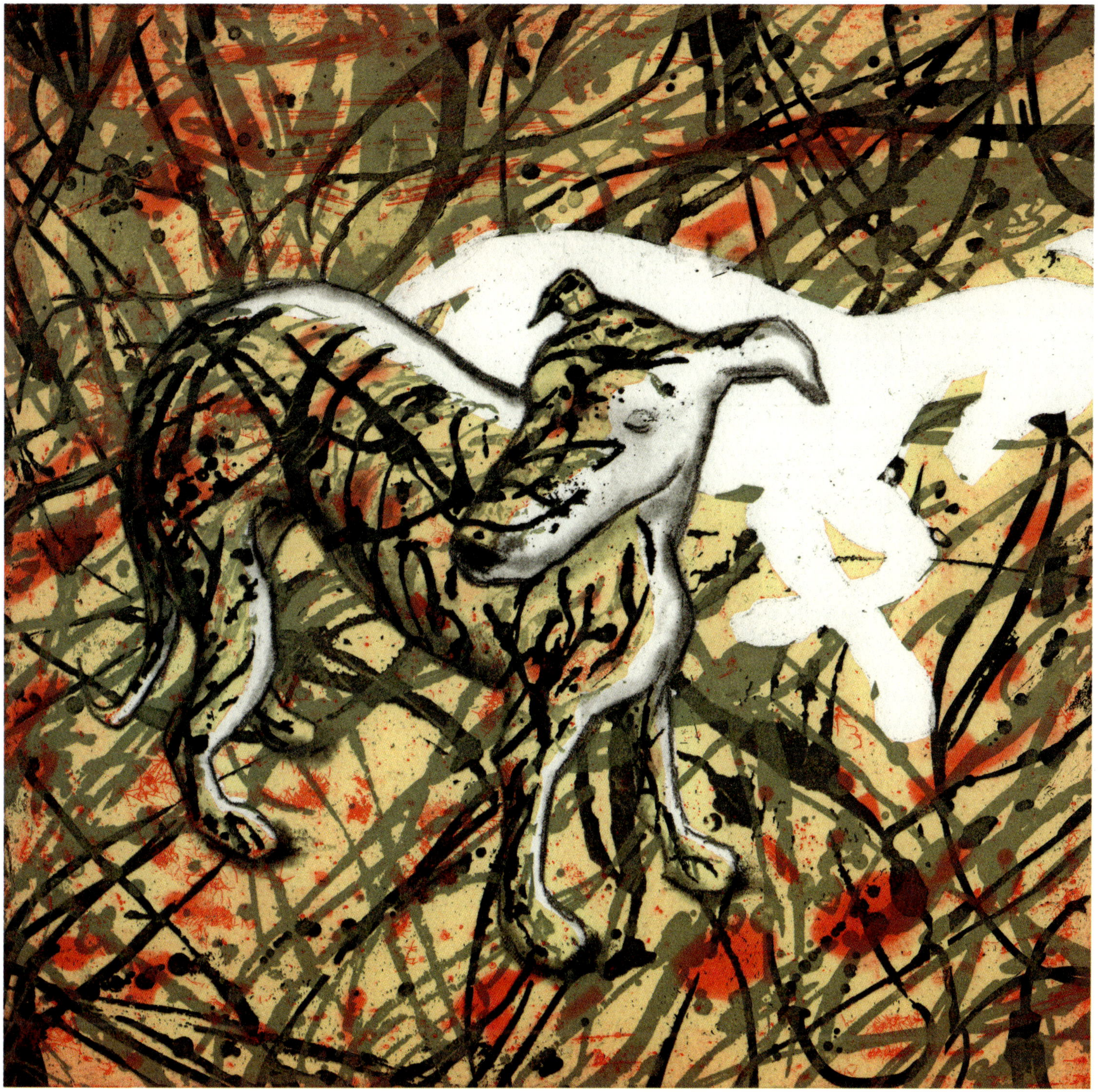

EDMUND DE WAAL'S DOG

Oil on panel
40 x 40 cm
2015

Edmund de Waal is possibly as well known for his wonderful book *Hare with the Amber Eyes* as for his beautiful ceramic installations. This combines the two and includes a portrait of one of the actual pieces from his collection of 264 Japanese netsukes.

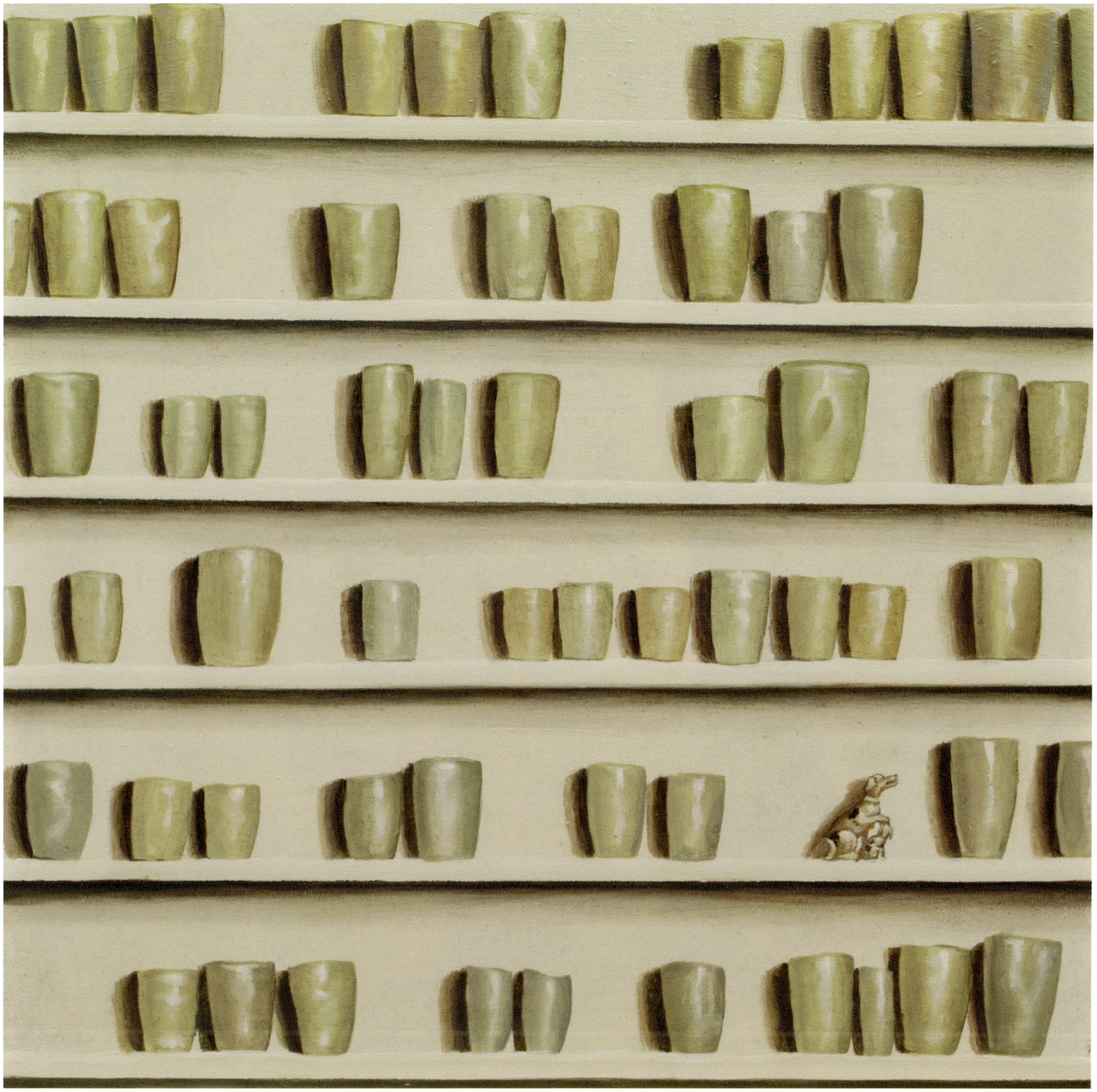

TURNER'S DOG

Oil on panel
40 x 40 cm
2015

The inspiration for this painting came while I was looking at Turner's *Burning of the Houses of Parliament*, however, the silhouette of the artist was taken from a still from Mike Leigh's 2014 film *Mr Turner*.

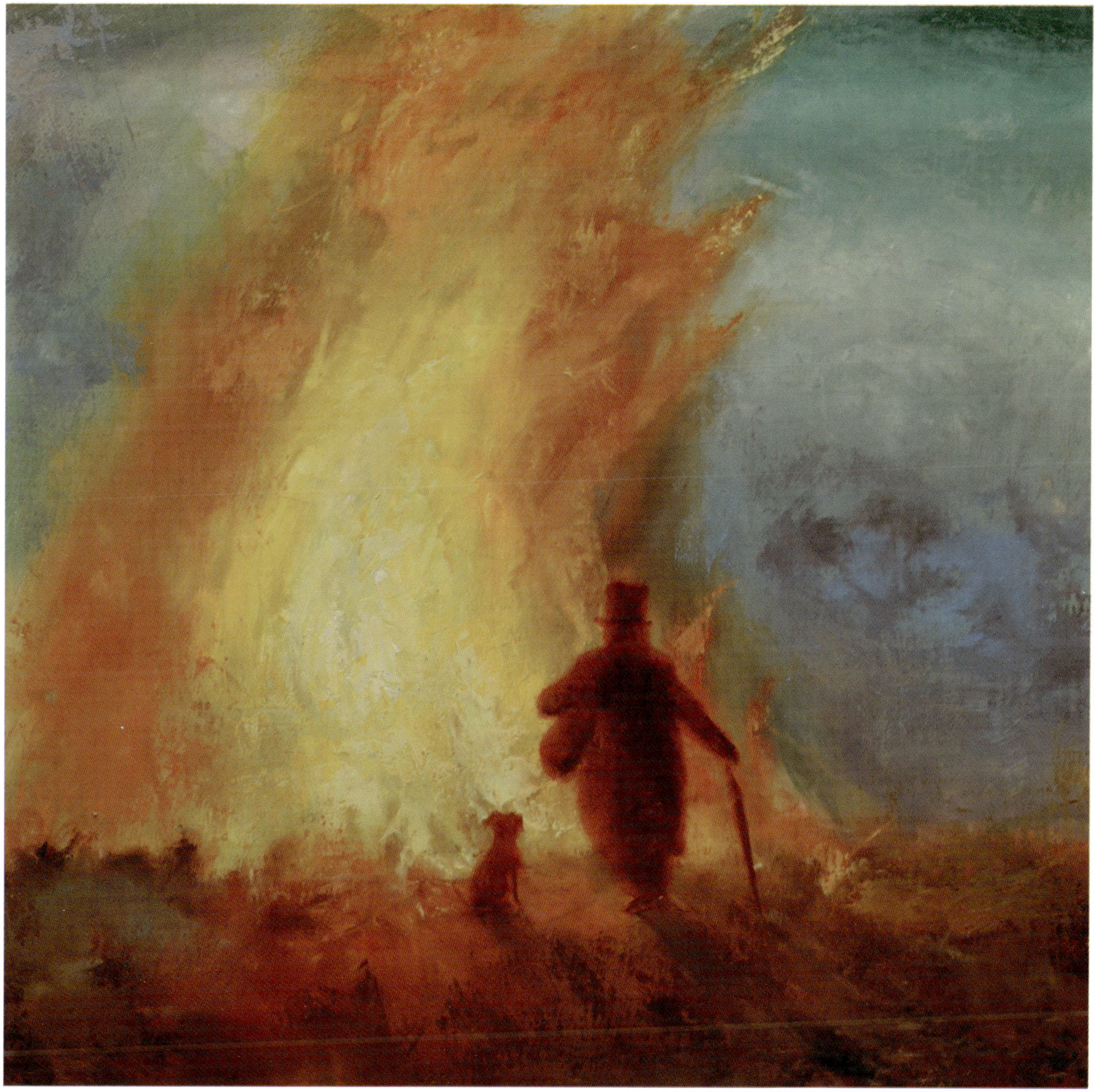

LIST OF ILLUSTRATIONS